FIRING FIDO!

How Radically Redefining Loyalty
Unleashes True Leadership
in Everyone's Work and Life

Chris Kozakis

TRAFFORD

FOR MORE INFORMATION ABOUT *FIRING FIDO!*
Consulting Services and Workshops for Organizations
U.S./Canada call toll-free: (866) 700-5113
International call: (602) 331-0334
www.FiringFido.com

National Library of Canada Cataloguing in Publication

Kozakis, Christopher T., 1963-
    Firing Fido!: How Radically Redefining Loyalty Unleashes True Leadership in Everyone's Work and Life/
    Christopher T. Kozakis.
    ISBN 1-4120-0565-5
    I. Title.
    HD57.7.K69 2004   658.4'092   C2003-903399-6

First Edition

This book has not been prepared, approved or licensed by any entity that created or produced *Cheers*™, *Chicago*™, *Contact*™, *Cool Hand Luke*™, *Disney*™, *Fiddler on the Roof*™, *Fram*™, *Gilligan's Island*™, *I Love Lucy*™, *Maude*™, *Mommie Dearest*™, *My Big Fat Greek Wedding*™, *Office Space*™, *One Flew Over the Cuckoo's Nest*™, *Our Gang*™, *Pinocchio*™, *Pogo*™, *Scooby-Doo!*™, *The Godfather*™, *The Music Man*™, *The Odyssey*, *Warner Brothers*™ or *What About Bob?*™.

TRAFFORD

This book was published *on-demand* in cooperation with Trafford Publishing. On-demand publishing is a unique process and service of making a book available for retail sale to the public taking advantage of on-demand manufacturing and Internet marketing. **On-demand publishing** includes promotions, retail sales, manufacturing, order fulfilment, accounting and collecting royalties on behalf of the author.

Suite 6E, 2333 Government St., Victoria, B.C. V8T 4P4, CANADA

Phone	250-383-6864	Toll-free	1-888-232-4444 (Canada & US)
Fax	250-383-6804	E-mail	sales@trafford.com
Web site	www.trafford.com	TRAFFORD PUBLISHING IS A DIVISION OF TRAFFORD HOLDINGS LTD.
Trafford Catalogue #03-0934		www.trafford.com/robots/03-0934.html

10   9   8   7   6   5   4   3

Dogs don't lie, and why should I?
Strangers come, they growl and bark.
They know their loved ones in the dark.
Now let me, by night or day,
Be just as full of truth as they.

-- Garrison Keillor

All the examples referenced are actual events that occurred.
Names, locations and identifying details have been changed.

Firing Fido!
CONTENTS

The Final Tail

Barking Up The Right Tree

Last But Not Leash (Appendices)
      plus: ...Share It With Others
              ...About The Author
              ...Want To Know More About Organizational Transformation?
              ...Want To Know More About People Transformation?
              ...Acknowledgments
              ...Notes
              ...No Dogs Were Harmed In The Writing Of This Book!

Author's Note

This book is about how most people sacrifice their own needs for the sake of something or someone else. The title is *Firing Fido!* and I chose the dog theme since dogs represent the qualities of devotion, attachment and loyalty to the extreme. I like dogs but it just wouldn't have worked as well with cats, parakeets or howler monkeys!

So what exactly is a *Fido*? *Fido*, for the purpose of this book, is overloyalty or misplaced loyalty to a person, belief or habit. This lopsided loyalty causes performance and satisfaction to suffer. It gets in our way of getting what we need in our careers and lives.

Webster's Dictionary defines loyalty as being 'faithful to a person . . . cause, ideal, custom, institution or product'.[1] In this book, I expand this definition to include loyalty to other things we come into contact with in our daily lives (i.e., habits, departments, titles, etc.). Most people think they can't be loyal enough and that loyalty is the way to ultimate security and success.

I'm redefining that old, unhealthy definition of loyalty to mean 'becoming aware of our own *needs* and making the meeting of these *needs* our primary priority'.

I'm specifically using the word *needs* rather than *wants*. *Needs* can be defined as needing to live, to love, to learn, to belong, to be cared for, to be cared about, to be recognized and to be treated with respect. *Needs* are our basic rights as human beings and people can define their own needs any way they wish. These things are not *wants*, however, such as 'I want a million dollars' or 'I want everyone to worship me'! *Wants* are simply our own desires. **The real problem is when we become more devoted to what other people *want* than what we *need*.**

Dogs, by nature, are overloyal to their human masters and, in their obedience, surrender themselves completely. A dog will go for a walk on a hot day, whether it's good for him or not, because he feels the master wants to walk. A dog will walk to the point of exhaustion. People, in much the same way, can share this fate when they become overloyal in their careers and lives . . . never questioning these loyalties can be *just* as unhealthy.

I believe we need to undergo a **radical redefinition of loyalty in order to unleash our true leadership**. This may sound counterintuitive but my experience has shown that loyalty, in the way it is often used, actually gets in our way of taking responsibility for what is rightfully ours. Radically redefining loyalty is the way to make our jobs and lives more enjoyable - to be able to do more creative, productive and energetic work.

This book is, by business standards, quite intimate. I hope you will find this unusual crossover between living and leading to be intriguing, integrative and helpful. This is a *new* vision that can be used to build your confidence and enable you to reach your goals. In these pages you will find what you *can't* learn from Peter Drucker about living and won't learn from M. Scott Peck about leading!

The book is grounded in proven business fundamentals and healthy therapeutic principles of behavior. As you read the book, please apply it to your life as appropriate to your situation. While most of the examples are situated in the workplace, the principles can be applied to many life situations as well. I hope you will share the book's message with others - especially the people closest to you, the ones we usually find most difficult to deal with openly. One day I hope to give this book of life lessons to my own sons or daughters to aid their life journeys in becoming healthier and happier people.

I would like to acknowledge the many clients, co-workers and friends whose actual real-life stories (along with my own) appear anonymously throughout the book. Names and circumstances have been altered to avoid identification and to preserve the confidentiality my profession requires.

I offer a few words of thanks to some of the literary guides who provided inspiration for my own life and career journey, including M. Scott Peck, John Bradshaw, Melody Beattie, Margaret Singer, Joseph Campbell, Tom Peters and Peter Drucker.

As you read and incorporate these principles, my sincere hope is for you to become a true 'human being' rather than simply a 'human doing' - in order to make a life while you're making a living. You only have one life - it's your choice how you live it. Jack London said, "The proper function of man is to live, not to exist." [2]

For all you dog lovers out there, I hope you will enjoy the theme of this book and come to recognize your own Fidos.

Now, go fetch!

Chris Kozakis
Phoenix, Arizona
January 2004

A PEEK INSIDE
THE KENNEL

Caged And Uncaged Fidos
(Obstacles you fully or partially control)

Nothing represents a loyal best friend quite like a dog. If this book were a manual for dog trainers, the first topic would be handling techniques used for any breed of dog. The typical tools and techniques a trainer uses to handle a dog are collars to restrain for training/disciplinary purposes and bones to reward. This book, however, is about people and how one of humanity's most treasured virtues, loyalty, can actually become an obstacle that gets in the way of people getting what they *need*.

Behaviors inside people will be divided into two categories: 1) 'Caged Fidos' are obstacles people wrestle with internally that they *fully* control (e.g., the company where they choose to work) and 2) 'Uncaged Fidos' are obstacles they *partially* control (e.g., who their leader is).

The master has full control over the caged dog, knows where it is and what it's doing. The dog may be noisy, messy and mischievous but it can't chew up the sofa when it's in the cage. The master, however, only has partial control over an uncaged dog. The dog may be running around without a leash and heeds the master's call sometime but not all the time.

Actual harm can be inflicted because the uncaged dog may also bite people.

By first dealing with the Caged Fidos people fully control, they'll be able to deal more effectively with the Uncaged Fidos they partially control. People usually cope with their everyday obstacles (Caged and Uncaged Fidos) in one of these ways:

- **Feeding Fido.** This is done by coping with, putting up with and encouraging the obstacle. The belief is that 'Fido should be tolerated'.
- **Fighting Fido.** This is an uphill battle that is rarely won. The belief is that 'Fido must not win'.
- **Fixing Fido.** This involves trying to make incremental changes that often result in insignificant improvement. The belief is that 'Fido will get better if people just try harder'.
- **Fooling Fido.** This results in people remaining in denial about the obstacle's impact. The belief is that 'Fido does not exist'.

This book offers a different alternative to provide revolutionary improvement, that is: ***Firing Fido!*** In other words . . . Buh-Bye Bowser, Catch You Later Canine and Sayonara Spot!

Overloyalty And Misplaced Loyalty

As mentioned in *Author's Note*, loyalty is defined as being 'faithful to a person . . . cause, ideal, custom, institution or product'. In this book, I expand this definition to include loyalty to other things people come into contact with in their daily lives (i.e., habits, departments, titles, etc.). Most people sacrifice their own *needs* for the sake of something or someone else. **I'm redefining loyalty to mean 'becoming aware of our own *needs* and making the meeting of these *needs* our primary priority'.**

A brief word about loyalty . . . I don't have a problem, per se, with loyalty. Loyalty to institutions such as our family and our organization is fine. These are the 'ties that bind' and keep our community cohesive. When people overdo loyalty, however, or place it where it doesn't belong - sacrificing their own *needs* for the sake of a person, belief or habit - they get into trouble.

Overloyalty is when people put the *needs* and *wants* of others ahead of their own *needs*, even if it's only 51 percent focused on others and 49 percent on themselves. This loyalty imbalance is a question of degree and doesn't have to be 100 percent on others and zero percent on themselves in order to cause problems. Even a slight imbalance can distort peoples' entire perception. This doesn't mean, of course, that people can abandon their regular, day-to-day responsibilities, such as providing for their families and meeting work requirements.

Misplaced loyalty is exemplified by having faith in a harmful ideology or substance to get us through the day. Even a one percent attachment to the wrong thing, such as heroin, can be very destructive. A full definition of terms is found in the Appendices (*Last But Not Leash*).

How To Have More F.U.N.

Many people collar themselves through overloyalty to their own self-limiting perceptions and behaviors, or to people to whom they are overly devoted. This obstructs their ability to take personal responsibility and accountability for what is rightfully theirs. This gets in the way, ultimately, of people getting the rewards they desire - having FUN and enjoyment in their work (the 'people equivalent' of *bones*). Everyone defines FUN differently and my definition of 'F.U.N.' is:

Firing (fido)
Unleashes
e**N**ergy

The most important benefit people gain from having F.U.N. is the intrinsic satisfaction of doing fulfilling, rewarding and enjoyable work that is linked to their true identity and what they do best. F.U.N. leads to more creativity, productivity and energy with far less fear and stress. Energy fuels action! This is not goofy, laughing-all-day-at-the-amusement-park kind of *fun* . . . this is the F.U.N. that gets good work DONE!

Healthy Confrontation Is The Key To F.U.N.

What's the tool used to obtain this blissful state? **People need to confront themselves and others in a healthy way.** First, they need to <u>fire</u> any bad habits to which they've become attached. Second, they need to deliver hard news to others in a truthful and respectful way when making tough decisions. Healthy confrontation is a requirement for honest and effective working relationships. The motivation for healthy confrontation comes from caring about people and wanting them to perform to their highest capability. It's about treating people <u>better</u> - that is, treating them fairly and respectfully. Yes, I realize that sounds counterintuitive - but it's true. *Most* people have it backwards.

Good working relationships involve mutual disclosure of information and trust. The goal is for us to know the other person and to let the other person know and understand us. The more we know about each other, the better we can work together (communicating our *needs*, listening and connecting) and the better decisions we'll be able to make. Communicating our needs, of course, should not be taken to the extreme of trampling on other peoples' feelings or being self-aggrandizing. Good working relationships are based on taking an honest and sincere interest in the other person - not phony backslapping.

A truly healthy working relationship is exhibited by a person telling others the truth as he or she perceives it and talking to the person in charge of doing something about a particular situation . . . as long as it's done in a calm manner and not as a personal attack. This confrontational truth-telling needs to be done in person and in private - not as a whistleblower to the press or an attack in public.

Most people incorrectly believe *any* confrontation is bad confrontation and ultimately leads to unhealthy conflict. A 'comfortable' relationship, however, does not necessarily mean it is healthy and honest. The traditional view most people have of a 'good' working relationship is one built largely on avoidance and denial. In other words - not telling the truth as they perceive it and doing anything except confronting! Lack of mutual and honest self-disclosure causes many people to remain in a state of ignorance about each other's *needs* and impairs their working relationships.

Making the tough decision to deal with a person is extraordinarily difficult for most people. It's foreign to how they were raised. Rather than directly addressing situations, most people were taught to cope, cover up and make excuses for others under the guise of *caring*. Their definition of caring was *to take care of*. Rather than risk speaking the truth as they perceived it and possibly offending a person, they took care of him in a way that caused him to become progressively ineffectual.

In the family I grew up in, we constantly made excuses to our friends and family about the insensitive behavior my father exhibited toward most of our relatives in Massachusetts. Although he has many admirable qualities, his overall treatment of our relatives is not one of his strong points - a trait he picked up from my grandfather Thomas (as will be described in the chapter *"The Dog Eats Steak!"*). While growing up, and even long into adulthood, we covered up and avoided healthy confrontation with my father concerning his treatment of others. We never learned how to establish healthy boundaries with him or others. We never knew what boundaries *were*, let alone how to establish them. (Boundaries are defined as how far we can go with comfort in a relationship.[3] They are guidelines to help people clarify the limits of acceptable behavior.)

Confrontation has developed a bad rap because it is often associated with unpleasant people - in our own lives, in film and on television. What comes to mind when you think of Bea Arthur in the 1970s TV sitcom *Maude*? Or Faye Dunaway as Joan Crawford in the film *Mommie Dearest*? Or Nurse Ratched in the film *One Flew Over the Cuckoo's Nest*? Do words such as domineering, overbearing and obnoxious occur to you? Confrontation does not need to be an 'all or nothing' game. The goal is to behave in the middle of the two extremes - to take the best of both worlds and avoid the worst of each. It's not a choice between no confrontation (constantly avoiding, denying, delaying) and using confrontation as an 'in your face' option. The goal is to confront others only when necessary.

Confrontation does not begin with confronting others on their performance issues. The majority of *Firing Fido!* focuses on peoples' confrontation with themselves - their own internal (both Caged and Uncaged) obstacles, self-limiting perceptions and behaviors. Many of these internal obstacles are unconscious and running on autopilot. Self-confrontation is required before ever confronting anyone else. The characters in the upcoming stories first address their own obstacles, the Fidos inside them, to get what they *need*. They free themselves from the chains of the collars restraining them to get the bones of F.U.N. rewards and enjoyment at work.

So get ready to learn how to shed your own collar and go after the rewards you deserve: increased satisfaction with work and life, more respect and more F.U.N. There are simply no bones about it!

Walking The Dog
(How to move around in the book)

Firing Fido! is organized into a series of separate chapters that can be read either sequentially or in any order you desire. Its easy-to-read style will result in quick application of the principles before the book has a chance to get dog-eared! Feel free to turn directly to the specific *Fido* chapter you believe is most relevant to you and your situation or experience.

Most (but not all) of the chapters contain the following basic subheadings:

- **Into The Doghouse**: The point at which trouble begins after the situation and characters have been introduced.
- **Fido Gets Fed**: The price paid for the overloyal behavior.
- **Fido Gets Fired**: The specific action taken to change a situation.
- **Paws To Reflect**: Key lessons - looking at the situation from an objective viewpoint - regarding both the productive and counterproductive steps taken. A great place to turn for quick tips and suggestions on how to address the issues discussed in the chapter.

- **Best Of Breed**: This statement summarizes the main point of the chapter.

A few chapters also contain the following subheading:
- **Further Paws**: Appropriate checklists or additional insights and lessons.

There are some variations to these subheadings based on the unique characteristics of individual chapters.

The stories in this book are true. As the saying goes, 'a pint of example is worth a gallon of advice', so I am sharing real-life situations to make my points. The stories are representative of common occurrences in organizations but I'm not attempting to describe every possible situation. In all cases, names and circumstances have been altered to avoid identification.

I use gender-specific language to lend authenticity. The message in each chapter, of course, is not aimed solely at a male or female reader. Have fun with what I'm offering and learn from the experiences of both genders along the way.

THE FIRST TAIL

"The Dog Eats Steak!"

If I have any beliefs about immortality, it is that certain dogs I have known will go to heaven, and very, very few persons.

-- James Thurber

My grandfather loved his dog more than anyone or anything else in the world. He loved him so much, in fact, that he fed him only boneless Prime Grade steak every day. That's Prime Grade . . . not simply Select Grade steak!

My grandfather's name was Themistocles Kozakis and his namesake in ancient Greek history established the harbor of Piraeus, linking Athens to the Mediterranean Sea. Athens soon became the center of merchant trade in the ancient world, which generated great wealth to a hardscrabble city-state. (The anglicized version of *Themistocles* is *Thomas*.)

Thomas died four years before I was born, unfortunately, so I never had the chance to meet him. This story is about his favorite dog - a black, white and brown beagle named Koupriti (pronounced coo-*pree*-tee). The story was passed down in my family and now I'm passing it on to you to illustrate some important principles.

My grandfather led a very rough and stressful life. He emigrated from Greece to the United States in 1905 at age 20. Eleven years later he married my grandmother Mercine and they had five children. She was a very joyful woman - the unofficial hostess of social activity for just about all the Greeks living in West Lynn, Massachusetts. People happily streamed through their home daily.

Mercine, tragically, died from pneumonia within a few weeks after catching a cold. She was only 33, leaving Thomas a widower with five children to raise by himself. At the time, his children ranged in age from six to 14 years old. He was heartbroken and sadness enveloped the entire family. My grandfather never remarried and bore his huge family responsibilities alone - worrying constantly and rarely smiling.

After the death of his beloved wife, Thomas' only joy and consolation in life was his dog Koupriti. He truly loved the dog and considered him to be his best friend. Koupriti was a devoted companion and a good watchdog who obeyed commands without hesitation. Thomas had peace of mind with Koupriti around. The dog had the uncanny ability to pick up on my grandfather's moods. They napped together on the porch almost every day - Thomas in the rocking chair with his lovable beagle's head on his lap.

Thomas treated Koupriti like royalty. He gave more attention to the dog than he did his own family. He often visited nearby Loomos' market to buy Prime steak for the dog. He bought steak for his own family to eat only once every three weeks but the dog ate steak every day! Thomas gave Koupriti a bath every three days and the veterinarian gave the dog a physical exam every six months rather than just a regular annual checkup. Koupriti always comfortably slept inside the house at a constant temperature of 70 degrees Fahrenheit.

My grandfather was a loner and had few close friends. He had a much better relationship with his dog than with people. He preferred being with Koupriti because the dog didn't talk back or harbor any personal agendas. Thomas was honest and sincere but he was also extremely opinionated and lacked discretion when dealing with others. Rather than exchanging pleasantries when he met people, he immediately confronted them if he didn't like something they said or did.

Thomas worked many years for the General Electric Company and retired with a good pension. He enjoyed his retirement by going hunting or fishing every day with Koupriti. He and his dog spent half the year in the U.S. and the other half in Greece to cover both hunting seasons. After World War II, Greece's economy was in ruin - no jobs were available and there was mass starvation. Greeks were scrounging for weeds, roots and berries - then boiling and eating them - to survive.

While in Greece, Thomas paid premium prices on the 'black market' to buy steak for Koupriti. The Greeks were starving and he still fed his dog steak! His dirt-poor relatives and neighbors went crazy. His brothers screamed, "For the love of God, Thomas, what are you doing? We're starving here and you're feeding the dog steak!" The criticism didn't bother Thomas in the least. My grandfather, unlike his historical namesake *Themistocles*, was not overly concerned with the economic struggles of the Greeks of his time. He insisted that Koupriti would live as comfortably in Greece as he did in the U.S., replying, "The dog eats steak!" He told his relatives collectively to go fly a kite (it sounds much nastier, of course, when said in Greek)!

Thomas had many tough breaks during his life and both his love and affection for Koupriti were admirable. The dog, however, didn't care what he ate - he just wanted to be with Thomas and fed well. My grandfather's attachment to Koupriti had turned into *overloyalty* - his priorities were out of whack and he was blind to the consequences. The result was a series of unhealthy confrontations, which had a negative impact on relationships with important people in his life.

If Thomas hadn't consciously fed the dog steak while other people around him were *starving*, then he could have made it easier for others to develop a deeper and more rewarding connection with him. He could have had more harmonious relationships with his relatives and he might not have been such a loner. My grandfather could have lived a more enjoyable and fulfilling life.

I inherited many wonderful things from my family but some aspects of my inheritance were unhealthy. They were handed down through many generations of 'Kozaki' and embedded in our DNA. They felt intractable by the time they got to me. While I never fed a dog steak during an era of severe economic depression, I inherited some of the overloyalty characteristics my grandfather displayed. These traits became obstacles in my life.

The following sections of the book describe real-life situations of clients, co-workers, friends and mine. I'll describe how obstacles got in our way and were addressed. It seems we've all had things in our lives to which we've become overattached. For my grandfather, it was Koupriti . . . for the rest of us, we'll call them *Fidos*.

CAUTIONARY TAILS

How To Deal With Caged Fidos
(Obstacles you FULLY control)

So what exactly is a *Fido*? It derives from the Latin word *fidus*, which means faithful or loyal. *Fido*, for the purpose of this book, is overloyalty or misplaced loyalty to a person, belief or habit. This lopsided loyalty causes performance and satisfaction to suffer.

Following are the tales of caution for things to guard against - all the obstacles in peoples' way. Self-limiting perceptions and behaviors inside people constrain most of them from getting what they *need* in their careers and lives. As mentioned in the chapter *Caged And Uncaged Fidos*, the stories will be divided into two categories: 1) Caged Fidos are obstacles people wrestle with internally that they fully control (e.g., the company where they choose to work) and 2) Uncaged Fidos are obstacles they partially control (e.g., who their leader is).

Over the next series of chapters, the stories will describe specific situations where unconscious loyalty needed to be examined, scrutinized and redefined - rather than simply accepted at face value. Loyalty, per se, is not bad. People get into trouble when they overdo loyalty or place it where it doesn't belong - sacrificing their own *needs* for the sake of a person, belief or habit. Loyalty is not being eliminated. I am simply changing the way people think about it.

Let's begin with the Caged Fidos - the obstacles people wrestle with internally that they fully control. The first one will be the fixation on security.

When Your Fido Is...Fixating On Security

In the whole history of the world there is but one thing that money can not buy . . . to wit - the wag of a dog's tail.

-- Josh Billings

The 1970s musical group *The O'Jays* sang so soulfully, "Money, money, money, money . . . MONEY! . . . For a small piece of paper it carries a lot of weight." [4] The preoccupation with *security* is one of the major obstacles for every person on the face of the earth. Overallegiance to security focuses on fear of the unknown rather than on the available choices. An operating system of fear runs in the background of many peoples' decisions. It's like a hungry dog waiting at the kitchen door and it knows that the door will be left unguarded at some point. Most people are anxious about their lives in general and the uncertainty each day brings, so they focus disproportionately on perceived security. These fears are heightened by pop culture and what the media portrays as 'real life'. Turn on the local television news any evening to see an ongoing series of fearful disasters. The underlying message is that the boogeyman is around the corner - watch out! It's a powerfully unconscious thought process.

Security is whatever others dangle in front of individuals that people think will improve their lives and safety. Rather than considering a multitude of options to pay the bills and have F.U.N. in their lives, many people put too much emphasis on some of the tenure-based benefits they receive from their employer such as insurance, pension and a 401K plan. They will guard against any change by ensuring these things stay exactly the same. People can also feel like hostages to their home mortgage - the house owns them rather than the other way around.

Many people hang on for dear life to jobs they hate for 20 or 30 years simply to maintain company benefits. They use their desire for *security* as a way to abdicate responsibility for not having any choices in their careers, or not doing what they really desire to do in their lives. People need to realize, however, that they can control this belief rather than letting it control them. Overattachment to security is a smokescreen many people use for not confronting whatever is in their way. They simply don't want to confront their lack of confidence in themselves, or 'rock the boat' with their spouse, or are unable to deal with an issue they have with their leader. It's <u>never</u> solely about the money - it's about what their priorities are and what's important to them right now. It's what they're willing to invest in themselves and the risk they're willing to take on their own talents.

Although the fixation on *security* is <u>fully</u> controllable by people, many Fido stories, both Caged and Uncaged, have security concepts interwoven. These include chapters such as:

- *When Your Fido Is...Juggling A Family Business And Ethics* (Caged)
- *When Your Fido Is...Lacking A Work/Life Balance* (Caged)
- *When Your Fido Is...Overidentifying With A Title, Role Or Profession* (Uncaged)
- *When Your Fido Is...Peacekeeping With A Spouse Or 'Significant Other'* (Uncaged)

Let's start by looking at one of the primary Caged Fido chapters focused on security: *When Your Fido Is...Overdependence On The Organization.*

When Your Fido Is...
Overdependence On The Organization

Brothers and Sisters, I bid you beware
Of giving your heart to a dog to tear.

-- Rudyard Kipling

Lyle was an Engineer at LockhardTech, a large firm based in Maryland that created electronics. He was a conscientious, diligent worker and a devoted father to his two children. Lyle was the sole wage earner in his family and wanted to provide for them as well as possible. He felt obligated to give his children the educational and financial opportunities he never had while growing up. Similar to many long-term employees who entered a firm thinking, "This is the company I'm going to remain with for a long time," Lyle went to work and got into a comfortable groove. He was well paid and promoted on occasion.

Lyle, like many people from the Baby Boom generation, focused on working his way up through a corporation and maintaining constantly challenging jobs with some level of prestige. He thought he was punching his ticket on the success train by working numerous nights and weekends to get ahead.

The values of the Generation X and younger folks, however, revolved around working in an enjoyable and more casual workplace - having the freedom, flexibility and training to obtain marketable skills for the overall job market. Lyle often frowned upon their emphasis on freedom, flexibility and enjoyment. He relied instead on the implied social working contract that worked well in his father's day (1950s-1970s): work for a solid firm, be loyal to the organization, keep his nose to the grindstone and 'don't rock the boat'. His father taught Lyle to believe that the firm would take care of him by providing job security for life and a nice pension.

Into The Doghouse (the trouble begins)

Lyle burrowed like a groundhog and focused his attention on working hard at his job in the company. He assumed that as long as everything was going well in his department and in the company, then he would be safe. His friends often warned him, though, not to become complacent and rely so heavily on company stability and job security. Lyle pondered their advice but believed his lack of a graduate degree limited his earning potential at any other company. In his mind, the only way he could provide his children a top college education was to stay with the same company and work very hard. He was so single-mindedly focused on getting his children into certain universities that he held onto a job he could barely tolerate for many years.

There was a huge shift, however, in the implied social working contract that Lyle had been taught to believe. The corporate struts beneath him turned out to be built on shifting sands rather than bedrock. After working 20 years for the company, Lyle was laid off due to a corporate restructuring. Most of the engineering jobs were moved to India due to its large pool of highly educated, qualified and relatively low wage employees. This stood his entire world on its head - the whole social working contract changed and every assumption he worked under was blown apart. Lyle's job security and affiliation to the group of people he worked with for 20 years was gone. Gone! He still had his pension funds, however, and the technologically current knowledge gained from his work experience.

Fido Gets Fed (the price paid for overloyalty)

The company's implied social working contract tended to create a culture of entitlement and to perpetuate a sense of employee dependency on the firm. Companies often attempt to improve their benefit programs to attract good talent and make themselves a more desirable place to work. It is a slippery slope, however, from that situation to 'we will take care of you'. Human beings are wired to seek comfort. Most people hearken back to when they were children and dinner was on the table when they got home from school - home was a warm, dry, comfortable and secure place with food. These patterns are very traditional and tough for most people to resist.

...Bitterness Paralyzes Lyle

In Lyle's mind, the company had broken the social contract and he felt a sense of real betrayal. He didn't know how to react to this major change. He was caught completely unprepared, was bitter and lashed out by blaming others for his situation. Lyle told everyone, "I'm getting screwed! I can't believe the company did this to me after all the hard work and long hours I put in. This damn company owes me big time - I gave them everything I had. Is this the thanks I get?" He was really afraid he would never be able to get a similar job with another company that paid him as much. He felt stuck and his anger and pain quickly degenerated into paralysis.

...Lyle Fails To Network

Lyle didn't realize he never really worked for an organization - instead, he worked for and with *people*. Those people moved from organization to organization over time, thus creating his potential network in many organizations rather than simply one. Lyle, however, did not entertain multiple ways of applying his skills and knowledge. He failed to network. It was fine for him to be loyal to his organization and have pride in his company while he worked there. His problem occurred when that turned into overloyalty. He was unable to move elsewhere successfully and let go of the past. To quote Walt Kelly's comic strip character *Pogo*, "We have met the enemy and he is us." [5]

Paws To Reflect - Counterproductive Steps (key lessons)

Lyle's intentions were good, of course, and he wanted to provide well for his family. Like many people, however, his core problem was that he never asked himself the question - "Who am I and what do I need?" - to determine what he was really trying to accomplish in his career. Lyle evolved into his current situation in life through a series of somewhat random occurrences. Suddenly, he said to himself, "I've got a good deal going here - I want to keep what I've got." Then the corporate restructuring occurred. The real question is, "What did Lyle really have?" He had never identified his true natural gifts - his strengths and talents. He had never asked himself, "What are my values, ethics and principles? What can I live with and what can I live without?"

Lyle made the mistake of equating *comfort* with *safety* - believing that as long as he just hung in there, then everything would turn out fine. Rather than being responsible for his own career, he gave his power away to the company. Lyle became overattached to the status quo and hung on for dear life to the *illusion* of security he expected the company to provide him.

FIRING FIDO!

Paws To Reflect - Productive Steps (key lessons)

Lyle was collared in his career by determination, duty and commitment to one firm. The behaviors he should have focused on initially were direction, desire and compatibility:

- <u>Direction</u> is more important than determination.
- <u>Desire</u> is more important than duty.
- <u>Compatibility</u> is more important than commitment.

This doesn't mean, of course, that Lyle should have abandoned his regular, day-to-day duties and responsibilities, such as providing for his family and meeting work deadline requirements. The best approach for him would have been to focus <u>first</u> on getting his proper overall career direction, then on working hard. That way, the tail would not wag the dog. Determination, duty and commitment to the organization were only valuable to the extent they were aligned with *his* direction, desire and compatibility. Lyle discovered the hard way that simple determination, duty and commitment were not getting rewarded in today's world the same way they were in his father's world. He should have focused on these three steps:

1) Become aware of what he was best at and enjoyed doing - to understand his own true natural gifts.
2) Decide to find a company that valued his true strengths.
3) Develop the confidence to move outside his comfort zone and act on his decision.

One of the possible outcomes of applying the *Firing Fido!* principles is that an employee such as Lyle would become an even better and *more dedicated* employee. If he had first clearly determined <u>who he was</u> and <u>what he needed</u>, then he could have joined an organization consistent with his true identity and needs. Instead of having his entire identity tied to his work, he could have worked at the company out of a sense of choice for that entire time rather than out of

obligation. There is extraordinary power in choice and focus.
If Lyle chose to stay, then the firm would have gained the
benefit of an even better employee - more committed and
dedicated toward the company and its causes. He could have
done better work and had a whole lot more F.U.N. at what he
did. His energy would have fueled his action!

Lyle was responsible for awareness of two things: 1)
aligning his job with his true natural gifts and 2) understanding
the stability of his company within a global economic context.
Alignment with his true natural gifts would have removed
some of the risk and fear he felt when changes occurred. Lyle
didn't realize that *true* security was tied to the full use of his
talents. Letting go of loyalty to outdated beliefs would have
unleashed his true leadership and provided him with even more
security, stability and safety. The job market is always better
for people who are good and know how to communicate their
value. If Lyle had taken care of his own needs first, then he
could have taken better care of both himself and the business,
because the business didn't necessarily take care of him in the
manner he expected.

Here is what I would say to Lyle if I had the chance:
*"You were compensated fairly for your work. All you owed the
firm was your conscious effort for the time you were at work -
to be focused on delivering excellent service to your customers.
All the company owed you was a paycheck every two weeks
and to treat you with dignity and respect. That was the deal -
so every two weeks you were even. The contract was fulfilled.
The company owed you nothing. You owed the company
nothing."*

Best Of Breed:
*Loyalty can often be attached to something outdated.
Moving outside the 'comfort zone'
actually moves a person into the 'safety zone'.*

When Your Fido Is...
Overattachment To Family Beliefs

But was there ever dog that praised his fleas?

-- W. B. Yeats

Brett and Graham were best friends prior to going into business together. Brett founded and served as President of OptiMedical, a small biotechnology firm in California. Brett owned 35 percent of the company, other investors owned 45 percent and Graham, the Vice President of Marketing, owned 20 percent. Graham had created and overseen numerous successful marketing initiatives while in management positions for many large corporations. Brett assumed that Graham's marketing experience would translate well to a startup company.

Into The Doghouse (the trouble begins)

Graham, however, was simply not up to the task of driving a marketing initiative in a startup firm. This became clearly evident in a short period of time. Graham flew first class to a meeting in Hong Kong that had practically no chance of producing a sale. He also brought in a high-priced marketing firm and paid them to develop ideas for *unfinished* products. When questioned about any of those decisions, Graham simply replied, "This is how it's done when you're one of the big boys. This is how I did it in the airline industry and this is how I'm going to do it here!" Graham's performance dragged the company into the netherworld but Brett avoided confronting him.

Brett didn't disclose his frustration about Graham's underperformance to Graham himself or to anyone else inside the organization - but privately seethed over the situation. Rather than seeking advice from a career counselor on how to handle the situation most effectively, he made the mistake of asking his family for advice. They told Brett to do nothing and that the situation would work itself out. His family told him that if he confronted Graham, then his relationship would fall apart completely and Graham would never talk to him again.

Brett's parents and other family members, unfortunately, were the living embodiment of avoiding, denying, delaying and <u>never</u> confronting. They all had listened far too many times to the 1970s pop song refrain, "Don't rock the boat, baby." [6] Rather than directly addressing any difficulties, their entire approach to life was to just wait and trust that things would work out. Brett's family defined avoidance and non-confrontation as actually being moral behaviors. His family equated direct, straightforward and truthful confrontation with being evil, unethical and unfair. Oh, brother!

Fido Gets Fed (the price paid for overloyalty)

To keep the business moving forward, Brett not only did his own work but picked up many of the tasks Graham was supposed to do. Brett's hyper-responsibility caused him to work like a dog 70 hours a week, which resulted in an inordinate amount of stress and burnout. He had no personal life, often got sick and certainly wasn't having any F.U.N. at work. His energy level became dangerously low.

Brett decided to focus only on the positives about Graham's behavior and not bring up anything negative. By picking up most of Graham's tasks, he hoped that others in the company would somehow *magically* see that Graham wasn't doing his job. All this did was conceal the true problem, which was Graham's underperformance. Rather than focusing on Graham's lack of performance, Brett was more concerned with how he himself would be perceived. He had it backwards!

Brett's relationship with Graham worsened over time, due to his frustration over picking up after Graham and not making the tough performance-based decisions. Brett wasn't able to do his own job as well as he could have due to his overwork. In the end, the underperforming, yet politically savvy, Graham was able to muster a large enough coalition with the other investors to actually *oust Brett*. It was a sad ending to a good friendship.

Paws To Reflect - Counterproductive Steps (key lessons)

As well-meaning and loving as they may be, many families are usually not objective. Families are very reluctant to see children change and many families encourage children to keep doing the same old things they learned from the family itself. *Different* is often viewed as *incorrect* because it doesn't follow the expected 'family script'. Allegiance to following a family script is the most automatic of all the Fidos. Children had no choice in how they were brought up and taught to think by their families. The way people view the world - their system of beliefs and assumptions - is based to a large extent on their family script.

In spite of his direct life experiences to the contrary, Brett never challenged the basic beliefs he learned from his childhood experience. As an adult, he had the power to change the impact of the family script on his current actions. He unconsciously engaged, however, in self-defeating and self-sabotaging practices, and he let his family script control him. Although it wasn't intentional or malicious, his family upbringing made it extraordinarily difficult for Brett to take the proper action concerning Graham's performance.

Sometimes when a person such as Graham isn't very task-oriented, he may have sufficient interpersonal skills to head off problems before they occur. Graham, however, didn't possess that high level of relationship skill. The problems still occurred and had to be resolved - it's just that *Brett* had to deal with them. Brett, unfortunately, didn't confront Graham on either his lack of task follow-through or relationship effectiveness. Brett, like many people, had the greatest difficulty dealing openly and honestly with the people closest to him. Brett's covering up and taking on Graham's duties and responsibilities was a disservice, actually, to Graham. Implicitly, Brett told Graham it's perfectly all right *not* to do his job, not to meet standards and not to meet expectations. Brett deceived him and unknowingly treated him *unfairly*.

Change implies moving outside the comfort zone and Brett wasn't willing to do something he didn't like to do. Brett made the *Fatal Fido* error of leadership - he wanted to be liked and regarded as the 'nice guy' more than he wanted to be respected and regarded as the 'fair guy'. A Fatal Fido is a behavioral mistake that causes practically every other problem to get worse. Brett's family script negatively impacted him in the workplace as well as in other situations in his life. Since he focused on being liked first, he lost the respect of everyone in the company. Brett, ironically, was liked by fewer people and was ousted. He didn't realize that healthy confrontation was the best way to care for others - the opposite of what his family had taught him.

FIRING FIDO!

Paws To Reflect - Productive Steps (key lessons)

Brett would have been perceived as being both nice and fair if he focused on gaining respect as his first priority. If Brett had confronted Graham in a healthy way, then he would have treated him <u>better</u>. Telling Graham the truth as he perceived it would have been the highest form of respect. Healthy confrontation would have been motivated by compassion - looking out for Graham's best interest and welfare. Showing true respect for others meant not allowing a problem to fester and drag on beyond the limits of good sense.

Brett should have confronted Graham in a fair and healthy way - without blame or hostility. He could have called attention <u>quickly</u> to Graham's performance issues by explaining the performance standards and expected business outcomes. Brett could have been upfront, fair and honest by telling Graham the truth as he perceived it in a respectful and objective way. He could have asked Graham, "What do you think is the cause of the problem? How much of it do you think is your responsibility and within your control and what would you like to do about it?" If Graham agreed that a problem existed, then Brett could have allowed Graham to come up with improvement recommendations to correct his performance and move it to acceptable standards. He could have treated Graham as someone capable of change and improvement - giving him an appropriate amount of time to change. Brett could have persistently encouraged Graham through positive feedback - specific, constructive and to the point - and helped him take responsibility for his own performance.

If Graham had improved his performance to acceptable standards, then the situation would have improved. If not, however, then Graham should have been removed from his position. Good business is not a popularity contest.

On the family front, Brett needed to challenge certain unhealthy family beliefs. He could have taken three productive steps to reduce his attachment to self-defeating beliefs:

1) Brett solicited his family for advice. They didn't force it on him. Rather than accepting their advice at face value, however, Brett could have asked them, "Have you ever tried that course of action with someone? If so, please tell me how it worked and why it worked that way. Did you ever try another alternative? If so, please tell me how it did or didn't work and why." He could have determined if their advice had been *proven* to work or was simply being handed down blindly from prior generations.

2) Brett could have talked to trusted people outside his family (who didn't know his family members), or a good therapist, to perform a reality check on the advice his family gave him. Family belief systems are, by definition, usually insulated from significant outside verification. He needed to gain a different perspective to determine if his family's advice was a functional approach to dealing with his situation.

3) Brett could have learned about healthy and unhealthy family dynamics by reading books such as *Cutting Loose* by Howard Halpern,[7] *The Family Crucible* by Augustus Napier with Carl Whitaker[8] or *Bradshaw On: The Family* by John Bradshaw.[9]

Best Of Breed:
People should question the way they were raised.
They should embrace the things that work well and
discard the parts that get in their way
of growing into even better people.

When Your Fido Is...
Juggling A Family Business And Ethics

Men are generally more careful of the breed of their horses and dogs than of their children.

-- William Penn

Reg and his brothers ran Arcadorama, a small video arcade business based in Massachusetts. Their father started the business as a pinball arcade and ran it on his own for many years. Reg earned a masters degree from a top business school and had a successful career for many years at a large brokerage firm. The time came for his father to retire and he wanted to pass responsibility for the family business to his sons. He called Reg and said, "We need you! We're running into some difficulties. You have the business background and the business management degree that I paid for. It's time to give back to your family for just a little while, until we get back on our feet." Reg, being a good and obedient son, grudgingly agreed to follow in his father's footsteps. Fifteen years later . . . Reg was still there!

Into The Doghouse (the trouble begins)

Reg was the Chief Executive Officer (CEO) of the family business in name only, since everyone received equal partnership compensation regardless of position or performance. What a disaster! Reg didn't have the mandate to take a full leadership role in the company, so the company couldn't hold him to a separate standard.

Growing up in Reg's family, the unconscious *family script* was 'everyone was the same' and 'do not stand out because to be different meant you were trying to be superior'. Reg grew up thinking he was only able to tell others what to do as long as it was what his brothers could do as well. He was hesitant to be seen as an elitist. Reg probably thought he grew up in Garrison Keillor's *Lake Wobegon*, "where . . . all of the children are above average." [10] The family failed to realize that *different* did not mean *better than* . . . *different* was simply different. In fact, Reg <u>was</u> different. He clearly displayed the best executive skill set in the family and deserved to be compensated for these differences. The family wanted to have its cake and eat it too. They wanted Reg's CEO skills but didn't want to threaten the family system by paying him more money.

Fido Gets Fed (the price paid for overloyalty)

The wives of Reg's brothers came into the picture and things worsened. They were accustomed to 'putting on the dog', driving expensive cars and living in upscale neighborhoods. They were risk avoiders and feared any change that threatened their status (as if staying the same involved no risk!). Large national chains recently entered the local market and used the latest video technology. Reg understood that innovation was required for the growth and prosperity of the company. He knew that standing still was a huge risk to take in a competitive marketplace. So he pushed to invest some company resources to buy the most popular video games. His brothers and their wives, however, looked at the business as a cash cow and refused to allow any additional investment. They planned to keep milking it until Elsie the bygone bovine belched out her last long, "mooooooooooooooo!"

Reg also wanted to make changes to the officers' compensation to recognize his CEO level of responsibility. Since he owned 33 percent of the company and his brothers together owned 67 percent, they told him, "There will be no changes." Reg became resentful and gave himself the subconscious message, "If everyone is going to get paid the same, no matter what they do, why should I go the extra mile?" He did not unleash his potential and the organization was deprived of his full CEO value. He was neither being accountable to himself nor the business. As Reg's enthusiasm for the job waxed and waned, the company began to go into a 'peak and valley' mode of good months and bad months.

Another complication for Reg was the situation with his brother's wife Rebecca and her unemployed, ne'er-do-well brother Ernie. Any job seemed to be *beneath* Ernie and he could never hold on to a regular job. Reg had tried to employ Ernie by opening a new video arcade branch on the other side of town and letting him manage the place. In only three months, however, Ernie ran it into the ground and the family had to sell it at a loss.

The company collected a large amount of cash every day at its primary arcade location. Certain family members took the cash from the arcade to the bank to deposit into the corporate account. On more than one occasion, Rebecca took about $8,000 in cash to the bank and claimed she, "lost the money along the way." The company filed a claim with its insurance carrier to recover the money but the carrier refused to pay and cancelled the policy.

Reg strongly suspected that Rebecca gave the money to her brother Ernie to help support him but he couldn't prove it. Since the family business was a private corporation, a public audit of funds was never required and the family buried the issue. Their accountant simply accepted the company's financial numbers at face value. Reg faced an ethical dilemma.

He was unwilling to confront his brother directly about his suspicion, so he talked to his father. His father said, "I'm not sure if what you're saying is true but Ernie has been in a tough spot lately. He's having trouble supporting his wife and two children, so we shouldn't be too hard on him. Let's look the other way on this one." The family business was bound more by loyalty to D.A.D. than to G.A.A.P. (Generally Accepted Accounting Principles)!

Reg realized both the family business and the family system were bigger than he was. When a good person works in a bad organization, the organization wins practically every time. The organization is bigger and more powerful than the most powerful person. Not only was the organization bigger than Reg, so was the family. Family history goes back hundreds of years and it's a juggernaut to struggle against. Reg wasn't struggling just with his brother, sister-in-law and father. He was struggling against the entire family system. Reg wasn't responsible for the fraudulent situation but he knew he would be smeared, if only by perception, if he stayed. This was the final straw for him.

Fido Finally Gets Fired (action taken)

Reg decided holding on to his self-esteem and dreams were more important than being part of the family business. He fired his Fido by resigning from the family business and starting his own consulting practice. Reg now advises family-owned businesses about how to take their companies to a higher level and avoid the pitfalls he encountered . . . and he's finally getting paid what he's worth!

Paws To Reflect - Counterproductive Steps (key lessons)

Reg did just about anything to avoid emotional confrontation or to threaten the family structure while he worked in the family business. Emotional confrontation is a major fear for many men - it tends to make them take cover and hide.[11] Even men who are good at making tough business decisions have an incredibly difficult time making tough personal decisions.

The two most critical decisions for management to make in any business are the hiring and firing decisions. Practically everything else flows directly from these two decisions - the result being either positive performance or negative fallout. Hiring and firing communicate the visible standards of acceptable levels of performance to everyone in the company.

It has been my experience that approximately 70 percent of all issues in organizations are due to ineffective hiring processes - the front door is broken! Around 20 percent of issues are due to not firing someone who should be let go and 10 percent are due to a variety of other reasons. In a family business, both of these major decisions are fatally flawed - the hiring decision is usually made more by nepotism than performance, and the firing decision is avoided at all cost. Performance issues are almost never resolved because firing a family member is usually not an option. Family members are rarely laid off when times get tough.

Once the hiring decisions are made, the next most important question to be asked in any business is, "Who is going to be the leader?" In a family business that question is almost never resolved adequately. Lack of leadership is one of the major reasons for small business failure - either by a lack of vision or a lack of consensus among the leadership team on how to execute the vision.

Most members of a family business are willing to overlook many things to meet their desire for group affiliation. It's all about guilt - what the family members think they owe each other due strictly to the accident of birth. Many people fear something worse than being fired - excommunication from the family. Exclusion is a pain worse than death.

Most people enter a family business because their family expects them to, not because it's what *they* want to do or are best at doing. Reg's father didn't say, "I want you to do what makes you happy and what you enjoy doing." Instead, his father implied, 'Do what your forefathers did and pay what you owe'. Many adults are 50 years old and still trying to make their parents proud of them. They fear risking security and family approval. Reg's allegiance and obligation to his family script caused him to lose some of his uniqueness and he unconsciously began to resent his parents.

Living a life of obligation to the family, rather than one of freedom and choice, makes it almost impossible for a person to stay true to himself, his own dreams and doing what he loves. It's not impossible for people in a family business to learn how to make requests of others and confront in a healthy way. It is *extremely* challenging to do so, however, since it's difficult for a family to let one family member be different. The price of staying is usually too high to both the business and to the family relationships. If a family business were truly run like a business, then the hard decisions would be made when necessary. A strong likelihood exists that personal relationships would be negatively impacted. If a family business were run more like a family than a business, then the cost to the business of coping with underperformers would be very high. The usual level of coping found in a family business often shatters the morale of the non-family members who are working for the company.

In a family business, protecting and preserving the family belief system becomes more important than people protecting and preserving their own selves. Most people bow down to what they perceive the family *wants* rather than what they themselves *need*. Any family member who desires to hold on to his self-esteem and dreams would be wise to follow Reg's ultimate example and **leave a family business . . . even if no ethical dilemma exists**.

If I were to write an entire book on the subject of going into a family business, it would be only ONE page long and that page would contain ONE word:

DON'T!

There, I've said it! Some family businesses, of course, are financially successful in spite of all these issues. The question, however, remains - at what cost to the family (if it's truly run like a business) or at what cost to the business (if it's truly run like a family). While some family businesses manage these issues more effectively than others, the core issues are often never truly solved - they can improve only marginally.

Paws To Reflect - Productive Steps (key lessons)

In a non-family business, leaders have the flexibility to apply effective hiring principles. They may be appropriately trained or gain the assistance of hiring professionals. Another good resource is *Hiring the Best: A Manager's Guide to Effective Interviewing* by Martin Yate.[12] It's easier, of course, to choose people correctly than to try to change them.

But let's be realistic! In a family business, the odds are strongly against professional hiring techniques being used to select family members for most management positions.

Entrepreneurship is a great concept but people should not hire family members. They should reap their own rewards and enjoy their own lives.

Best Of Breed:
The only way 'to' is 'through'.
Families that avoid problems will never resolve the true issues.

Further Paws - When Fido Is Fredo

Most family businesses have a *Fredo* who is protected at all cost. In the film *The Godfather*, Fredo (portrayed by John Cazale) was the helpless and confused eldest son of Mafia family boss Don Vito Corleone (portrayed by Marlon Brando).

A Fredo, in general, has very low self-esteem - he was never taught how to be independent or accountable for his actions in the real world. From a very young age, the Fredo assumes the family business will take care of his financial desires and he depends on that to make a decent living. The family knows the Fredo is useless to the business but they fear what would happen to him if he took another path. The family's main concern becomes how to keep the Fredo stable and employed. They give the Fredo unimportant 'make-work projects' to keep him out of the way and attempt to limit his dealings with customers to minimize damage.

Managing around the Fredo becomes more important than managing the business. The focus of the business revolves around trying to manage the lowest common denominator - the Fredo! Most families are willing to jeopardize the business before doing anything to hurt the Fredo. They certainly won't confront him on any performance issues that should be addressed. Fredo is Fredo - they're not going to change him. They simply protect the Fredo under the guise of 'we're all equal here'.

As Reg found out the hard way, both his brothers and the ne'er-do-well Ernie were *Fredos*. None had any incentive to deliver consistent performance, since performance was not linked directly to compensation. While he worked in the family business, Reg avoided confrontation even though their inaction dragged the company down. He hid behind his allegiance to the family, which superseded the good of the business.

When Your Fido Is...Lacking A Work/Life Balance

It's been a hard day's night,
And I've been working like a dog.

-- John Lennon and Paul McCartney

Diane was a Technologies Director in the Systems Development area for IntaMation, a large computer company based in New York. Diane had a strong work ethic and was willing to be worked to death - always happy to do it and almost grateful for the chance! She lived for her work and was known as the overresponsible 'go-to gal'. She put in an incredible number of hours to get the job done to *her* satisfaction. Everyone relied on Diane due to her high drive and conscientiousness.

Into The Doghouse (the trouble begins)

Earlier in Diane's career, she was responsible for monitoring computers during software testing. On the night of each test, she brought in a sleeping bag and *slept* under her desk so she could be awakened if a customer problem occurred. Diane's actions bring to mind a remark Emperor Hirohito of Japan made, commenting on how his life had changed after World War II, "You can't imagine the extra work I had when I was a god." [13]

Diane so overused her drive that she didn't run it, *it* ran her. In her mind, all she heard was 'get the project done and

39

get the product out to market NOW'. She tuned out the background noise of 'and, oh yeah, by the wayyyyyyyyyyyyyy, you need to take care of yourself, so try to find an appropriate work/life balance as well'. When she had a chance, Diane enjoyed vacation time spent at the shore and she earned enough money each year to pay for a nice houseboat on the lake along with jet skis and water skis. She felt most at peace while on the water. She felt a lot of guilt, however, when she was away from the office for a prolonged vacation.

The term *workaholic* carried a positive connotation in Diane's organization. Workaholism, however, is really an addiction - an addiction to work. Addictions are any processes, activities or substances that take over a person's life and control him or her. Many unhealthy consequences flow from addictions.

Work addiction is the last socially accepted addiction. It's as American as apple pie and is fostered and promoted by much of American culture and society. Interviews in many periodicals, such as *Ms.* magazine, have women saying of themselves, "I'm a workaholic and I love it!" It's simply impossible to picture another kind of addict, such as a bulimic, on the pages of a similar magazine being portrayed as *happily* saying, "Puking 10 times a day - I highly recommend it!"

Fido Gets Fed (the price paid for overloyalty)
Many work addicts are more effective at their job than at personal relationships, which they find difficult and anxiety producing. Some work addicts try to avoid the personal lives they <u>don't</u> have and some try to avoid the personal lives they <u>do</u> have. Work addicts feel most alive when they are deep into their work. The *fix* of energy is not the work itself but the adrenaline high that accompanies the work.

Work addiction allowed Diane to medicate herself and feel secure - to avoid dealing with the complication and pain of the aftereffects of her divorce. She didn't feel very good about herself. Diane did just about anything to avoid dealing with her feelings of anger, sadness and guilt. She feared her ability to handle these feelings, so she engaged in constant work activity to block them from bubbling to the surface.

Work addicts tend to create a constant crisis orientation, sometimes accompanied by large mood swings - fabricating unhealthy conflicts and fueling crises to produce excitement. They experience a letdown, actually, when not at work or thinking about work. For healthy people who are not work addicted, there are pauses between projects - time to rest, savor their success and spend more time with their family and friends. This calm terrified Diane because now she would have to deal with the areas of her life that were messy and not controlled by the work process.

Diane was doggedly determined, while at work, to book every minute of each day to avoid having any slivers of open time in her schedule. She considered unstructured time a pure waste and almost always skipped lunch. Her high stress levels left her feeling exhausted and as sick as a dog. Diane was always busy doing so many things that she never had time to reflect on the things she *should* be doing. This became her Achilles' heel. Speed kills - it's difficult for anyone to think clearly or creatively when constantly on the run.

Diane denied being a work addict whenever anyone significant in her life brought concerns to her attention. One of the definitions, of course, of being a work addict is remaining in denial about the work addiction itself. Funny how that works, huh? Denial is the basic defense mechanism of addiction - if something doesn't exist, then it doesn't need to be dealt with. The bad news, however, is that the things people resist tend to persist and get worse over time.

Fido Doesn't Get Fired...And Not Promoted Either!
(action taken)

Diane wasn't being promoted as fast as she had originally anticipated. She was so busy doing all her tasks, as well as many of the tasks of her staff, that she didn't focus her efforts on communicating her accomplishments. Diane remained at her current level for a long time. Most workaholics fail to make the time to communicate effectively because they are so buried in accomplishing their endless series of tasks.

Paws To Reflect - Counterproductive Steps (key lessons)

Diane's intentions were good - she wanted things to go well and obtain good outcomes for the company. She never took responsibility, however, for the fact that unconscious overallegiance to her work ethic actually *impaired* her desired career advancement. Yeah, yeah, you might be thinking . . . "Life isn't fair." Well, as Jodie Foster said in the film *Contact*, "Funny, I've always believed that the world is what we make of it."

Diane wanted to do excellent work and that was perfectly all right. When, however, the 40-45 hour workweeks became consistently 60 and higher in order to meet 'above and beyond' excellence, she moved into the danger zone. The philosopher William James termed Diane's behavior akin to serving 'The Bitch Goddess Success'.[14] All Success wants is more . . . and it is a Bitch. Diane worshipped Success and it ran her life. Management experts Tom Peters and Nancy Austin wrote:

> "We have found that the majority of passionate activists who hammer away at the old boundaries have given up family vacations, Little League games, birthday dinners, evenings, weekends and lunch hours, gardening, reading, movies and most other pastimes. . . . We are frequently asked if it is possible to 'have it all' - a full and satisfying personal life and a full and

satisfying, hard-working, professional one. Our answer is: No. The price of excellence is time, energy, attention and focus, at the very same time that energy, attention and focus could have gone toward enjoying your daughter's soccer game. Excellence is a high-cost item." [15]

Paws To Reflect - Productive Steps (key lessons)

Diane might well have received a promotion had she changed what needed to be changed to run the organization in a more effective manner . . . then influenced upward by communicating these contributions in an appropriate manner to people in power. Diane often said, "I don't have to blow my own horn and tell everyone what I'm doing because my work speaks for itself." As the sadistic prison warden Strother Martin, however, said to Paul Newman in the film *Cool Hand Luke*, "What we've got here is . . . failure to communicate!" Diane believed this lack of communication was the only pattern to follow. By never challenging this belief, she stayed trapped in this behavioral pattern.

Senior management was not going to *magically* understand Diane's accomplishments within a vacuum of information. This wasn't about inauthentic self-promotion where she would be making herself look better by putting others down. This was about authentic self-leadership. People who influenced upward more effectively and communicated what they *did* and *needed* were promoted at a much faster pace than Diane. Many of them had a healthier work/life balance as well.

In addition to improved communication, here are three ideas the *workaholic* Diane could have used to create better boundaries around work and still maintained high performance:

1) <u>Slowly</u> cut back on working hours by about five percent a month until reaching the healthy goal of 40-45 hours a week.

   - Diane could sneak up on the addiction and trick it into getting healthy by letting it believe that everything's fine. The struts beneath the addiction, of course, are being removed - but so slowly as to be almost unnoticeable.

2) Draw a pie chart, using common graphics software, of hours worked each week as a visual reinforcement of behavior.

   - Diane could ask one person to come to her every week and ask to see the chart. This is the reality check that holds her accountable to her commitment to reduce her hours gradually. Addictions work best in secret and in isolation. This approach raises them to the surface.

3) Create some downtime during the day, when in the office, by carving out a time that everyone could depend on her <u>not</u> being available.

   - Diane could draw a clock on a piece of paper with the hands pointed to 3:00 and put it on the side of her cubicle at 2:30 with the message 'I will be available at 3:00 - please feel free to see me at that time'. She could reserve that half hour each day to do whatever she wanted *except* answer phone calls and meet with people concerning her latest project. It would be her time to *think*. Other peoples' schedules, over time, would likely start to take this time into account.

Addictions can be either substance-related (such as alcohol, drug or smoking addiction) or process/activity-oriented (such as work addiction). A full listing of addictions and related support groups is found in the Appendices (*Last But Not Leash*).

Best Of Breed:
The world's fastest greyhounds
race only once every three days.
Even they require some downtime.

Further Paws - Top 10 Signs Of Work Addiction
(Working like a dog)

A person only has to exhibit <u>one</u> of these behaviors and he or she either is, or is on the way to, becoming addicted to work:

1) Says, "I'm going to start working less," but it never happens.
2) Says, "I don't do this because I have to - I can stop this any time I want but I choose not to," but it never stops.
3) Mercilessly criticizes and intimidates others due to unrealistic expectations.
4) Says, "It's all up to me" and "If you want things done right, you have to do them yourself." Creates unnecessary work due to extra quality checks caused by perfectionism.
5) Constantly tells employees *how* to do every task, in addition to *what* to do, because of preoccupation with control.
6) Sees everything in 'all or nothing' terms - unable to see other options and lacks flexibility.
7) Views asking for additional staffing or help as a weakness.
8) Feels like a martyr 'fighting the good fight for the company's cause' but resents lack of career advancement.
9) Believes that being 'just good enough' is *never* good enough.
10) Believes the illusion that things will get better if he or she simply works *harder.*

CAUTIONARY TAILS

How To Deal With Uncaged Fidos
(Obstacles you PARTIALLY control)

The stories now shift from the Caged Fidos to the Uncaged Fidos. As mentioned in the chapter *Caged And Uncaged Fidos*, Uncaged Fidos are obstacles people <u>partially</u> control (e.g., who their leader is, how other people treat them, teams to which they are assigned, etc.). These obstacles often constrain most people from getting what they *need*.

Let's begin with a common problem - how overidentification with a title, role or profession can become an obstacle.

When Your Fido Is...Overidentifying With A Title, Role Or Profession

A door is what a dog is perpetually on the wrong side of.

-- Ogden Nash

Wendy was a Technical Analyst at ArtiNetwork, a medium-sized firm based in Arizona that provided technical solutions for small and growing businesses. She produced excellent results, due to her great listening skills, and was able to translate technical sales jargon into an easily understandable language for customers.

In addition to her regular technical work, Wendy also engaged in 'stealth strategic advising' to people in positions of power within the firm. She had excellent visionary ability and was able to communicate well with company executives. They trusted her and easily opened up to her.

Into The Doghouse (the trouble begins)

Wendy consistently accepted somewhat low-level technical jobs in all companies where she had worked, so her good strategic ideas were never publicly acknowledged by executives. The few times she was invited to an executive planning meeting, she'd be quickly hushed due to her title. In reality, Wendy had numerous meetings with the Chief Executive Officer (CEO) and was instrumental in clinching the firm's largest sales deals. She even helped keep the company afloat during a difficult period.

Wendy's level, however, put the CEO in a very awkward position. Ideas do not [necessarily] follow the good thinking in an organization - ideas follow the power.[16] The CEO's personal pride didn't allow him to implement her ideas publicly or even acknowledge them as coming from her. If he discussed her ideas with his Vice Presidents, then he ran the risk of taking strategic advice from a person with a lower-level title. How would that make the CEO look? He would look as if he didn't know talent when he saw it, his organization was messed up and his Human Resources hiring practices were ineffective - that's how! Otherwise, why would a low-level Technical Analyst be setting strategy for the company when his Strategic Vice Presidents weren't able to do so?

After hearing Wendy's strategic ideas at the Arizona Headquarters, the CEO told her, "Keep up the good work . . . we'll get back to you," and then relegated her to the corporate Siberia of the Northern Region office. The politically manipulative CEO took Wendy's good ideas, reformulated them a bit with his own personal stamp and told everyone in the organization to execute *his* vision. Wendy became immensely frustrated and resentful. She felt like the barfly Norm Peterson on the 1980s TV sitcom *Cheers* telling the bartender Sam Malone, "It's a dog eat dog world, Sammy, and I'm wearing Milk Bone underwear!"

Fido Gets Fed (the price paid for overloyalty)
Wendy became strident and had a series of blowups. She alienated herself from her manager, her manager's leader and the other folks who were working at the proper levels for their skills. Wendy found herself <u>telling</u> them what they should do rather than <u>guiding</u> them to a conclusion using appropriate influencing and alliance skills. She earned a

reputation as someone with many good ideas - but a hothead who had to be kept on a short leash due to her blowups when her frustration level boiled over.

By unconsciously remaining bogged down in and overidentifying with her low-level technical role, Wendy never confronted her own insecurity. An inner script ran in her head telling her she wasn't good enough to be in a strategic role, because she didn't possess the 'proper qualifications'.

Wendy didn't have a college education and believed the right degree would have validated her strategic thinking skills. It didn't matter that her actual experience and ideas were better than anyone else's in the company - all that mattered was that *almighty* degree. Sheeeeeeeeeesh! Her *title* was the main issue that influenced most peoples' reluctance to listen to her, not her lack of a college education.

Without the right access or opportunity to contribute on a consistent basis at the strategic level, Wendy's true natural gifts were never on full display. She was unable to have F.U.N. at work - it wasn't giving her the internal happiness she craved.

Fido Gets Fired (action taken)

Wendy transitioned herself out of her job at the company and started an independent consulting practice. In this new professional role, her strategic ideas were much more easily heard, appreciated and implemented by her clients.

Paws To Reflect - Counterproductive Steps (key lessons)

Wendy's career strategy, while working as an employee for numerous companies, was both low-risk and low-return. She comfortably advised and consulted using her wonderful ideas and high-level strategic thinking skills. She then constantly second-guessed everyone else and never had to take responsibility for her actions. Wendy neither felt the heat nor took the hits of being held officially accountable if her ideas didn't work. She wanted to have her cake and eat it too! At the same time, she was never rewarded and given credit if her ideas did work.

By taking a series of low-level jobs with numerous companies, Wendy wasn't being responsible to her own career. She was overloyal to her self-perception of being simply a *Technical Analyst*. The companies were not actively trying to stifle Wendy. By entering the firms at a low level relative to her skills, however, it was difficult for her to rise to a higher and more strategic level.

Paws To Reflect - Productive Steps (key lessons)

A good way for Wendy to have avoided these pitfalls would have been to enter a firm at an appropriate level for her skill set. If she came in as a *Strategic Advisor* rather than as a *Technical Analyst*, then the role frustration would have been removed. People would have had increased receptivity to her ideas because they would have *expected* her to offer strategic ideas. Her title represented a set of expectations the company had of her and determined to a great extent how she would be treated. Wendy's other options were to move to a smaller company at a higher level to display her strategic skills, or to become an independent consultant - which she did.

Best Of Breed:
Truth telling starts with individuals confronting <u>themselves</u> with the hard and healthy truths.

When Your Fido Is...Overidentifying With The Department, Company Or Geographic Location

Thou called me dog before thou had a cause,
But, since I am a dog, beware my fangs.
                    -- William Shakespeare, *The Merchant of Venice*

      Marlene was a Director of Operations in the Bank Servicing Department for BancSoutheast. The company was a large firm based in North Carolina that provided credit card services to both banks and consumers (depositors).

      Bank Servicing was a separate department from Consumer Servicing and the company never invested significant resources into Bank Servicing. The department was often left with budgetary table scraps. Most corporate policies seemed to favor consumers over banks. Marlene always felt badly for the underdog in any situation and viewed the banks as the orphaned *mutts* within the company. She was an agent of change and constantly tried to make the operation run more efficiently. She felt part of an indispensable, special group that was chosen to keep the 'cause of the mutt' alive.

Into The Doghouse (the trouble begins)

      Marlene's department merged with a similar department in Nevada and all Bank Servicing was transferred to that location. Although there was an abundance of good job opportunities in the Consumer Servicing side of the business that remained in North Carolina, she agreed to move to Nevada to continue looking after the banks.

Marlene's leader in North Carolina, who was her long-time mentor, told her, "If you stay here, you will always have a job and you will always do well." Her intuition started channeling the song from the film *The Music Man*, telling her to, "STAY right here, I say, right here in River City." She was unwilling, however, to give up on her mutt and desperately wanted to be part of the *cause*.

When Marlene considered her proposed move from North Carolina to Nevada, she assumed the corporate culture was the same in both places. Au contraire, Pierre! Marlene didn't take the time to talk to her new leader in Nevada beforehand and ask herself the question, "Does he really believe in what I'm trying to do and will I be supported in any way?" Her dealings with the Nevada office over many years gave her the answer to this question loudly, clearly and in a million different ways. The answer was, "HELL NO!" Marlene knew the atmosphere in the Nevada office was deader and drier than its surrounding desert. It fit the description, to paraphrase comedian Robert Townsend, 'If you don't believe in the resurrection of the dead, then just look at this office at quitting time'.

Fido Gets Fed (the price paid for overloyalty)

Many people overidentify with the company or with a specific geographic location. In Marlene's case, however, she wedded herself to her department. The move to Nevada turned out to be a disaster. In spite of all evidence to the contrary, she believed she could change the corporate culture of the Nevada office. All the clues were there but she chose to ignore them.

Although Marlene graduated from the school of experience in North Carolina, she felt like a freshman all over again in Nevada. In North Carolina, the Bank Servicing

Department focused on change and growth and making results happen. The Nevada office tried to be as conservative as possible and minimized all risk - an environment that simply loathed change. Since Marlene thrived on being an agent of change, her fit into the Nevada culture was completely inappropriate. It was impossible to muster the support needed from senior management to adopt her proposed changes.

Fido Gets Fired (action taken)

Marlene was accountable for her actions and tried her best to make the Nevada operation run more efficiently but she was barking up the wrong tree. Her job for seven years prior to this was to help the sales force work more effectively with the Bank Servicing Department. Together they had developed appropriate compromise positions between the two areas that aided the company as a whole.

Marlene's new leader in Nevada, George, was new to his position. One day he gave the sales force a tough my-way-or-the-highway speech that 'the party's over and the days of compromising are finished'. Without checking with Marlene first, he laid down the law to the sales force like a new sheriff coming into town, effectively destroying seven years of her work. Members of the sales force glanced over at her during the speech with a stunned look on their faces that implied, 'What the hell is going on here? Are you agreeing with this guy? We thought we could trust you!' Marlene was furious and stared straight ahead.

After the speech, Marlene made a beeline for George and said, "We have to talk <u>right now</u>!" They went to George's office, closed the door to provide some privacy and sat down. Marlene said, "I put up with this at times from my old manager in North Carolina and I'm <u>not</u> going to put up with it now. What you said made me look like I was in total agreement with you. You made it seem like I had sold my constituents down the river. I'm going to tell you right now - I don't agree with you. You blindsided me and didn't give me a chance to discuss this with you ahead of time."

Marlene continued, "Maybe you can convince me of the soundness of your position and maybe you can't. You didn't even give me the opportunity to help manage the expectations of various members of the sales force prior to this meeting. I could have helped you communicate this new message in a way they would understand. I could have helped ease them into your new way of thinking but you made us both look bad. They will now fight us vehemently!"

George sat there and took Marlene's harangue like a five year old who had been sent to the woodshed. His lips were tightly pursed and he wrung his hands. He hemmed and hawed. After a few minutes of discussion, the meeting was over. Clearly, this was not a positive beginning to Marlene's tenure in George's department. The relationship between them never recovered from this initial misunderstanding.

After a couple of excruciatingly painful years, Marlene's Nevada-based position was eventually merged with another department within the organization. George had the authority to protect Marlene from displacement but had never forgotten the ill will generated during their initial encounter. He withheld his protection for her. Marlene was displaced involuntarily, eventually given severance and left the company.

The situation turned out fine in the long run for Marlene. She went on to create a successful management consulting practice, was much happier and made more money. Sometimes what people think is bad at the time turns out to be the best thing that ever happened to them.

Paws To Reflect - Counterproductive Steps (key lessons)

Marlene made the major mistake of ignoring her intuition when faced with the decision to move from North

Carolina to Nevada. Her fixation on the *cause* of the suffering banks superseded her inner guide. She was unconsciously overloyal to her department and servicing the banks. Marlene put the perceived requirements of the department ahead of belief in herself. **She felt her unique effectiveness was dependent on 'who her customer was' rather than on 'who she was'.**

The department, over time, had the subtle power to define how Marlene looked at herself. The department's goals slowly became her goals and the department's perceived limits of her abilities became her self-imposed limits. She gradually gave away her power to the entity in determining how she felt about herself. Loyalty to her department turned into Marlene's worst enemy. Her loyalty drove her to take a job that was truly not F.U.N. and she sacrificed her own career at the company. She didn't help herself and she didn't benefit the firm. Over 10 years of expertise, experience and contacts of a valuable employee walked out the door the day she left.

Marlene was correct in standing up for herself and letting George know how she needed to be treated and what she believed to be the best way to manage the affairs of the company. She quickly realized that her belief system, principles and values were very different from those of George and his department.

Marlene approached her confrontation with George, however, in an ineffective manner. She didn't build an appropriate relationship level to understand him, his needs and engender his trust. Also, she went into the confrontation while she was still *hot*. Her style and tone were wrong, so all George heard was her tone rather than her message. He felt attacked and became defensive. If Marlene's goal was to stay employed at all cost within the department, then her approach was not in her best interest. She played with fire but didn't understand the nature of the flame. She went in *hot* and didn't know with whom she was dealing.

Paws To Reflect - Productive Steps (key lessons)

Marlene should have waited until the next day to have her discussion with George. She couldn't wait, however, until she was totally *cold* about the issue either. It's best to confront someone when *warm* - still having strong feelings about the issue - but not *hot* or *cold*.

When contemplating career moves, people first should take a 'fearless self-inventory' of their own needs. They can then use that knowledge to help them evaluate job openings and career opportunities more effectively. When considering moving from one department to another, Marlene should have documented the pros and cons of both her current area and proposed location. Fully understanding what she was potentially getting into would have helped her make an informed and balanced decision. She should have reviewed the entire picture to determine if her personal style would be a good match, because the bad match swallowed her up. As John F. Kennedy said, " . . . those who . . . sought power by riding the back of the tiger ended up inside." [17]

Best Of Breed:
Self-leadership is more important than loyalty.
If people consciously choose to put their own needs first,
then focus on the needs of the department or company,
both they and the company are better off.

When Your Fido Is...
Overrelying On Company Dogma

The poor dog, in life the firmest friend,
The first to welcome, foremost to defend.
-- George Noel Gordon, Lord Byron

Luke, an independent consultant, designed a hiring process for a department of NatDatum in Ohio. The company was a large firm that provided information systems for its customers.

As part of the hiring process design, Luke included the opinions and views of all major executives, including the Vice Presidents of Sales, New Business, Product Development, Business Operations and Technologies. Will, the Chief Financial Officer of the firm, was also one of the executives.

Into The Doghouse (the trouble begins)

Luke set up an appointment for a meeting with Will to review the design. He brought along Jenny, a Human Resources representative, to ensure full team understanding. At the appointed time, they walked into Will's office and Luke said in an upbeat manner, "Hi, how are you doing today?" Will said nothing, glanced down at his watch and sighed, as if he hoped the meeting would have been cancelled. Will, Luke and Jenny sat down at a conference table at one end of Will's office.

After everyone was seated, Luke continued, "We're here to talk to you about what you feel would make up the primary successful behaviors of a high achieving employee." At that moment, Will barked, "Stop right there!" He got up from his chair, walked back to his desk and picked up a small laminated card.

Will stalked back to the table and *flipped* the card so it skittered across the table and landed in front of Luke. Will looked at Luke and said in a challenging tone, "Do you know what this is?" Luke calmly replied, "Yes, I've seen it. It's a small card that contains the 10 principal company values and is distributed to everyone in the firm." Will continued, "Well, have you read it carefully?" Luke replied, "Yes, I've seen it and I've read it." Will thundered, "Perhaps you should read it again because in it we refer to our employees as *associates*! We take this very seriously. It's our number one value. We see ourselves as equal contributors to the cause and we adhere to that."

Luke remained silent as Will continued his righteous diatribe, "It's an insult to our associates when you refer to them as *employees*. I don't know what company you're from but we don't walk around here holding onto titles. We don't think, just because we have a certain title, we know more or better than anyone else."

Jenny glanced at Luke with a look of embarrassment on her face that implied, 'We knew this guy was bad but not *this* bad!' Luke sat silently and thought, "What a hot dog. If Will really believed in these values, he wouldn't be using all this 'holier than thou' crap on me! When is this guy going to start our discussion about excellent performers in his department?"

Will resumed lecturing, "This Values Card is what I live by. I don't think this meeting is going to be very valuable because *everything* that goes on in this firm is listed on that card and I subscribe to it 100 percent. So if you want to know what I think, then you should just read that card."

Luke composed himself and calmly replied, "Thank you, we understand. At the same time, we're sure there are some experiences unique to you, where you have come across someone who has, in your opinion, been a superstar. We would really appreciate your opinion about what you saw that particular person do to make him so exceptional." At that point, Will harrumphed, sputtered and finally began to describe one person in his area who did fit that description.

Fido Gets Fed (the price paid for overloyalty)

Luke was *eventually* able to pull the requested information out of Will but it was excruciating. Will used his allegiance to the Values Card not only as a smokescreen but as a wall to avoid discussion of any kind. Will relied on the Values Card to do his thinking for him. By avoiding any debate, he avoided taking any personal accountability for his own beliefs and the organization was harmed by his counterproductive behaviors.

The Values Card was a corporate tool that was agreed to and accepted by everyone in the company. Many people, in addition to Will, failed to apply the values appropriately in the context of particular situations. They used the Values Card as corporate gospel from which they numbly quoted chapter and verse that explained *everything* - a sacred guide for action. They gave lip service to the words on the card but became even more manipulative, which aggravated the company's backstabbing environment.

Members of the management team could appear as if they were all marching to the beat of the same drummer, when they might as well have been members of different armies going off in many different directions. The Values Card got in the way of any true discussion. It created the illusion of unanimity. Rather than the intended effect of aligning behaviors, the Values Card actually concealed performance issues and unprofessional behaviors.

Many exercises in company dogma have the same illusory effect. Values statements are representative of many efforts on the part of companies to communicate behavior and attitude expectations. These efforts can include such things as creating corporate vision, setting company mission or communicating organizational goals. These efforts, by themselves, are certainly not counterproductive. They become a problem, however, when they prevent people from learning, questioning, challenging and growing.

Paws To Reflect - Counterproductive Steps (key lessons)
Like most corporate dogma statements, the Values Card went unchallenged. It was off limits to any open discussion and became a label to hide behind. No one ever committed the political suicide of daring to question it publicly. Without a handy-dandy Values Card to point to, Will would risk exposing his own beliefs and experiences. These disclosures, of course, could have put him at odds with other members of management. Will didn't know whom Luke had talked to in the company while designing the new hiring process. He only knew that Luke had talked to many of the top company officers. Blind allegiance to the Values Card gave Will an easy way out in order to appear consistent with everyone else.

The company propped up laminated 'values stands' on everyone's desks and put up 'values wall posters' everywhere - which were then quickly ignored by employees. Most of the values posters were on the walls so long that when they were removed, the paint underneath was a different shade from the rest of the wall - and that's simply from the effects of fluorescent lighting! Laminated values cards ended up in men's wallets and women's briefcases, only to be used as windshield ice scrapers in the winter or to jiggle open hotel room doors.

Lamination deadens the values by giving the appearance they are carved in stone and helps to create a process that can paralyze productive change. **Corporate dogma tends to stop many people from thinking and causes organizations to calcify**. Corporate strategies and tactics are constantly evolving and require active participation.

It's fine for a company to decide on a guiding set of values and principles to communicate employee behavior and attitude expectations. The good intentions of Will's company, however, backfired due to overreliance and dependence on dogma statements. Results worsened. The firm failed to ensure the values were truly embedded in peoples' behaviors through an ongoing review of performance. The company didn't have the processes in place to ensure people were hired and promoted for demonstrating productive behaviors and removed for exhibiting destructive behaviors. All corporate change begins with people changing their own behaviors. Peter Senge wrote, "Organizations learn only through individuals who learn. Individual learning does not guarantee organizational learning. But without it no organizational learning occurs." [18]

The content of values statements is usually fine. The intent is to change and reinforce positive corporate cultural behaviors. Statements, however, don't change culture. Individuals change culture. What causes most of the resistance is when people see others being rewarded and recognized for behaviors that are not in alignment with the stated values. Hypocritical and dismissive behavior not only makes a mockery of values statements but thwarts their effectiveness.

Paws To Reflect - Productive Steps (key lessons)

Here are three quick steps the company could have taken to keep the values relevant and avoid 'value-card-itis':

1) Keep the Values Card unlaminated.
   - Putting the card on thin, onionskin paper would be a great *symbolic* improvement or, at least, including a revision date in the corner so that everyone would know when it was last printed.

2) Give people permission to question the company values.
   - People are then more likely to experience the values rather than simply believe them through blind faith. Both people and organizations learn and grow through healthy debate and constructive criticism.

3) Incorporate into the company values any important new developments in the economy or new market conditions.
   - Timely input keeps the values fresh and alive. Otherwise, companies become like Tevye in the film *Fiddler on the Roof* singing, "Tradition!" while the world is changing all around them.

Best Of Breed:
Company dogma needs to be replaced
with actively thinking people.

When Your Fido Is...
Overidentifying With The 'Gang' Or Team

I have always thought of a dog lover
as a dog that was in love with another dog.

-- James Thurber

Eric created TemporaryNet, a small startup firm in California that provided a way to broker temporary help services over the Internet. He began running the business out of his house and absolutely loved the esprit de corps he established from the very start. His wife brought coffee and donuts every morning for him and his 'gang', and they all enjoyed hanging out together. Even though the working hours were incredibly long, their feeling for each other made it all worthwhile for Eric.

Eric was an entrepreneur at heart - a 'start it up' kind of guy rather than a 'maintain it' guy. As the company grew, he moved the company into an upscale business office. He decided to bring in Roger, his long-time mentor who had impressive management experience from the automobile industry. Roger became the Chairman of the Board while Eric served as President.

Into The Doghouse (the trouble begins)

Roger and Eric, unfortunately, made the mistake of not laying out an official organizational structure to clarify their respective roles to the employees. After a few failed attempts at creating an organization chart, they decided it would simply impose an artificial limitation on a small company. As a result, no one understood the pecking order of who was in charge and under what circumstances the Chairman should be brought into the decision-making process. Due to the overemphasis on 'let's all just get along', the entire issue of 'who's in charge' was overlooked. After a few months, however, it was Roger who asserted his leadership role as the true alpha dog in the organization.

Roger brought in, over time, a bunch of his cronies from the automobile industry. Soon the company culture split into two distinct camps. Roger's camp came from the 1950s 'old school' style of management. Fraternizing with employees was deeply frowned upon and managers left the office early on Fridays to play golf together. Eric and his group, however, had an independent and entrepreneurial mentality, where the team worked hard and played hard. They thought nothing of staying up until the wee hours of the morning developing an innovative technical system change and ordering out for pizza.

People in the organization soon started following two different business strategies due to the split camps. Sometimes members of Eric's own team didn't agree with a decision he made. They would go to Roger's camp to see if he would adjust a particular idea and then go back to Eric with the changes . . . and vice versa. The employees were like children running to Mom when they couldn't get what they wanted from Dad.

Fido Gets Fed (the price paid for overloyalty)
Eric knew problems existed because critical technical system components and marketing ideas he wanted implemented were stalled and in some cases killed by Roger and his camp. He was annoyed but he didn't make waves. Everyone in the firm knew Eric backed down eventually from

confrontation. Although he got upset with his team for going to Roger behind his back, the next night it was all smoothed over and forgotten. He'd have pizza and beer with the 'techie gang' and tinker with the '*neato*' technology at an all-night 'bull session'. Eric might as well have joined Spanky, Alfalfa and Buckwheat from the 1930s comedy series *Our Gang*, climbed up the tree house, and put the 'no girls allowed' sign out front!

The company lost valuable time, unfortunately, while the two top dogs struggled for domination. Customers were lost and productive employees left the firm. Eric realized the company's direction was slipping away from him due to the conflicting vision of the two camps. Even though the company was floundering, however, no one ever 'rocked the boat'. All the agendas were kept under the surface. Everyone simply co-existed and coped for a long time.

Fido Gets Fired...Sort Of (action taken)

Eric finally decided to take on a more assertive role. He wanted to lead the organization by executing his vision. He also wanted to observe the reaction to his new behaviors by the other executives in the firm. Eric started to pull up his britches, step out and exert some of his influence by doing the things he should do as the leader. Sparks began to fly between Eric and Roger as well as between Eric and his old team. Everyone immediately became very uncomfortable. The team said, "Why are you doing this and challenging Roger? We just want you to go back to the way you were and everything will be fine."

Eric quickly discovered Roger did not trust him to be President of the firm. To Eric's chagrin, there was room for only one alpha dog in the organization. An important principle of alpha-dogness is the first dog on the block who establishes dominance in a role tends to keep it. Everyone knew Roger was the leader by the 'scent marks' he had left. When Eric tried to establish himself as the leader, he was viewed as an interloper dog trying to invade Roger's territory.

If Eric had stepped out and asserted his leadership role from the very beginning, then he may have been able to implement his vision for the company's services. The firm's operations probably would have run more smoothly. The opportunity, however, was lost. Eric waited too long to make these changes and he never regained momentum.

Fido Gets Fired...For Real (action taken)

Eric was eventually able to see the truth for what it really was in that organization - he was never going to be the alpha dog. It became obvious that he should leave the company. When he tried to establish himself as the leader, the backlash was swift and the coup was rapid. Roger was able to muster a large enough coalition to oust Eric from the organization, even though Eric owned the largest individual share of stock.

In the end, the ouster was the best outcome for Eric. He was forced to realize he hated trying to maintain and grow an existing organization. He just tried too hard to do what he wasn't best at doing. The role Eric truly loved was to be an inventor - to start up new companies and then leave the management to someone else. He moved on to create another successful startup company.

Paws To Reflect - Counterproductive Steps (key lessons)

Eric overidentified with the gang. He avoided taking a true leadership role because being part of the team was more important to him than leading the group. He didn't tell others what he really wanted because he feared being ostracized from them. Eric's motivation was to be accepted as 'one of the guys' - to be looked upon as an equal. He unconsciously thought establishing himself as the leader would come across as being 'better than' and 'superior to' everyone else. The gang is concerned with conforming to the group's rules and principles.

Although the team concept is a very powerful and positive one, teams can become tightly knit and insular - more allegiant to each other than to the good of the business. Some teams have a tendency to become dangerously rigid and they close ranks to defend the status quo.

Eric couldn't stand the thought of feeling alone. His loyalty to group affiliation limited his ability to make executive decisions. Eric was not fair - he constantly treated people like buddies and pals, displayed a lot of favoritism and cut them a lot of slack. His desire to be part of the team affected his ability to treat people in an equitable fashion.

Eric didn't realize that once he stepped out of the group and said, "I am the leader," there was no going back. He made the *Fatal Fido* error of leadership - he was more concerned with being liked first and respected second. Eric did not have the true authority to lead because he didn't make some of the tough calls and decisions. He wasn't fully accountable to being the best he could be in his executive role, so he wasn't being fair to the firm. Eric should have left the company, actually, long before he did.

Paws To Reflect - Productive Steps (key lessons)

Leading is understanding how to make the tough decisions and confronting in a healthy way when necessary - it's about commitment and decisiveness. The essence of leadership is to say directly, visibly and publicly, "Here's what we're going to do and why," do it, and then tell people, "Here's what we've just done and these are the results we accomplished." True leaders have the ability to step out, mark a new path, give direction and say, "This is the way, follow me." A leader is always in front and ahead of the rest of the team, if only by a little. The leader, by definition, is always a bit alone - not only from the rest of the team but from any other pretenders to the throne.

It's terrific for leaders to connect on both a personal and professional level with their staff - go out to lunch together, go out for drinks after work once in a while, and play sports and other activities. Employees are more willing to walk over hot coals for a leader who sticks up for them - one they respect, like and know - rather than one who is standoffish and distant. The leader who tries to straddle this fence, however, must be scrupulously fair with all his employees. A true leader holds everyone's feet to the fire when necessary - especially the people with whom he 'chummed it up' the night before.

Best Of Breed:
People have to be willing to give up something
to get something.
They need to give up being 'one of the gang'
to be considered true leaders.

When Your Fido Is...Peacekeeping With A Spouse Or 'Significant Other'

*When a man's dog turns against him
it is time for his wife to pack her trunk and go home to mamma.*
                                                                -- Mark Twain

Nick worked at a variety of management positions for over 20 years at LockhardTech, a large technology company based in Maryland. As part of a corporate relocation, Nick moved his wife Kay and three children from Maryland to Colorado. Kay preferred Maryland but agreed to the move for the sake of Nick's career advancement.

Five years later, Nick left the corporation to start his own independent consulting business. He ran his entrepreneurial endeavor for three years and was very successful from a financial standpoint. Nick had always done well financially, being the sole wage earner in his family, but his entrepreneurial business did not provide him the balanced lifestyle he craved.

To take his business to a new level of success, Nick worked with a career counselor on a regular basis over many months to develop a revised business model that met both his career and life goals. He analyzed all the activities he desired in order to be happy in his daily life and determined that he couldn't do all of them if he worked more than 20 hours a week.

Nick required a significant source of passive income to meet his three primary goals: 1) to return to Maryland eventually, 2) to work a maximum of 20 hours a week and 3) to travel out of town a maximum of 25 percent of the time. He had an overall life goal of having 'peace of mind, serenity, calmness and a simple life'. Nick consciously developed a plan, for the first time, that encompassed all parts of his life - a realistic business plan to do work he truly enjoyed that met all his goals. The plan provided for his family's financial security and relocation to Maryland within about one year.

Into The Doghouse (the trouble begins)
Spousal concerns, however, got in the way of Nick's plan. Many times over the previous eight years, whenever Nick promised to work on a plan to return to Maryland, he got sidetracked and it never came to fruition. Kay felt that taking another year to move back to Maryland was unacceptable.

Nick developed his career path around his three goals but Kay was operating by a different set of criteria. Her two goals were: 1) <u>immediate</u> geographic relocation to Maryland and 2) keeping their children in the same high school once they started. Kay assumed the family had enough in savings to fund the move and all related expenses.

In general, the communication between Nick and Kay was good. They sought the guidance of a marriage counselor to deal with any issues in a healthy way. Nick kept Kay constantly informed of his work with the career counselor and the revised business model they created. Kay, however, didn't trust Nick to follow through on his promise to move back to Maryland. Nick wasn't comfortable committing to one specific decision - he always wanted to keep his options open.

Both Nick and Kay agreed on the ultimate goal - to move to Maryland. It was simply a question of timing. In Kay's mind, if the move was delayed another year, then it would never happen. Kay told Nick her firm desire to move to Maryland was to be able to enroll the children in their new high school prior to the next fall semester. Although a direct ultimatum wasn't given, she implied the move would happen <u>very</u> fast.

Kay's mind was made up for a very valid reason and Nick realized this. He wanted to please her with regard to the extremely aggressive timing of the move and nervously agreed. As Queen Latifah sang in the film *Chicago*, "When you're good to Mamma, Mamma's good to you." He and his family moved to Maryland before their Colorado home sold and prior to Nick establishing his new business approach.

Fido Gets Fed (the price paid for overloyalty)

Nick's business in Colorado had always done well financially and now he was concerned how quickly he could establish a new client base in Maryland. He worried about the impact the frantic cross-country move would have on his efforts to start his business in a new state and feared not being able to make the amount of money he desired in the short term.

Nick's and Kay's monthly living costs doubled once they arrived in Maryland. They paid duplicate home mortgages, since their Colorado house didn't sell for a long period of time after they moved. They drastically lowered its selling price in a desperate attempt to sell that dog of a house. Their temporary housing costs in Maryland were much higher than originally anticipated. In addition, it cost over $50,000 to move their family across the country and enroll their children in an expensive private school. This didn't even take into account the fact that one of their children was only two years away from starting college and education costs were not yet completely funded. The entire family endured an incredible amount of stress during this relocation.

Kay even said she was willing to delve into their *retirement* funds to pay the monthly bills rather than delay the move one additional day. This added to Nick's concerns regarding money. An objective observer of this situation would say this was as far from having 'peace of mind, serenity, calmness and a simple life' as possible! According to many psychologists, many people are willing to accept almost any financial and logistical struggle to have a more harmonious relationship with a spouse.

Kay actually had an extraordinary amount of confidence in Nick's ability to succeed in his career and meet all his personal and business goals. In the short term, she viewed the immediate geographic relocation as being more important than allowing a business situation to develop quickly in which he could spend the amount of time he desired with his family.

Nick's new business in Maryland became successful after a period of time. His money issues became less of a problem but not without *a lot* of headaches along the way. He enjoyed doing this new kind of work but the overly aggressive timing of the move delayed him from meeting all three of his initial goals. Nick has not yet been able to gain a majority of his income in a passive fashion in order to live a balanced life, although he may be able to accomplish that goal in the future.

Paws To Reflect - Counterproductive Steps (key lessons)
Nick and Kay made the situation more complex than necessary for his business due to the incredible time crunch of the move. To their credit, they sought the guidance of a marriage counselor and did more work on their marriage than the typical couple. Many couples don't even take *that* very important step. Even so, Nick never fully trusted his own intuition and his fears caused him to give his power away constantly to others. Rather than examining his own beliefs to

determine what made him happy, he overrelied on the opinions of others - his wife, marriage counselor, career counselor and friends - in making his decisions.

According to many psychologists, couples often use a distraction such as a move across the country to 'feel new again', 'have a fresh start' and 'put the other stuff behind us' - which covers up any true underlying issues. Nick's and Kay's incomplete resolution of one of their key relationship issues - her lack of trust in him - caused a great deal of spousal fear and brought up control issues. Nick freaked out when he had to delve into his savings to relocate to Maryland. There are certainly more effective ways to manage a business than potentially jeopardizing children's college education funds and risking retirement accounts.

In the assessment of his career counselor, the fallout from the frantic cross-country move definitely got in the way of Nick's ability to accomplish the maximum business success in the quickest and most effective manner possible. The career counselor also felt Nick made the mistake of unconsciously letting circumstances determine his actions rather than having his strategy drive the events.

According to the consulting expert Hubert Bermont, "A laser-like approach to the building of your [consulting] practice without diversion or distraction is primal." [19] In most relationships, one spouse or 'significant other' can have a profound impact on her partner's work decisions and what he desires to get out of his career. (The genders in the previous sentence, of course, could be altered.) Compartmentalizing the issues of a marriage separately from the issues of making career decisions is a mistake. As Stephen Covey wrote, "Put first things first." [20] Nick and Kay used a marriage counselor appropriately and worked on their marriage relationship issues before working on career issues. They still weren't able, however, to completely prioritize and separate the marriage issues from the career issues.

Paws To Reflect - Productive Steps (key lessons)

In the opinion of his career counselor, if Nick had resolved his key underlying marital issues prior to exploring various career options, he could have gained clarity and been able to focus all his effort on his new business to create the overall lifestyle he desired. Nick then could have decided what his business was going to look like, determined his business goals and zoomed toward them like a greyhound in a much easier and more efficient manner.

Here are some suggestions on how people, in general, can deal more effectively with a spouse when it comes to making career decisions. Prior to meeting with a career counselor:

- First: *Realize* the true issues are often marriage relationship issues and not career issues.
- Second: *Together*, see a marriage counselor to completely uncover and resolve any major underlying relationship issues.
- Third: *Listen* to each other's needs. Write them down and exchange notes.
- Fourth: *Negotiate* a compromise. One person would get some desires met and the other person would get some desires met. No ultimatums allowed - veiled or otherwise. Winner does not take all!

Best Of Breed:
Overallegiance to 'keeping the peace'
can turn a best friend into a worst enemy.

When Your Fido Is...
Allowing Yourself To Be Undermined

Youth will be served, every dog has his day,
and mine has been a fine one.

-- George Borrow

Vince worked at BlancheCard, a large financial services company based in San Francisco. The reporting relationships in this company were as follows:

- Vince's leader, Ben, was the Director of the Customer Servicing Division.
- Vince was the Manager of the Collections Department in the Customer Servicing Division. (Vince reported to Ben.)
- Mario was the Supervisor in charge of certain customer accounts. (Mario reported to Vince.)

Vince had only been in this job for two months, although he had reported to his Director, Ben, for many years in a variety of other positions. Vince had a great deal of admiration and respect for Ben as both his leader and mentor. They were good friends.

Into The Doghouse (the trouble begins)

Ben had been the Manager of the Collections Department, years before, and unconsciously found it difficult to let go of his old area. Vince had asked Ben on countless occasions to teach him certain collecting techniques but Ben never found the time to review them with him. Ben often worked around Vince and directly called Mario, the long-time Supervisor in charge of certain customer accounts, to give Mario pointers about working an overdue account. Ben didn't mean to upset or undermine Vince - it was just the way he had always done it. Rather than orienting Vince properly to the new area, Ben was comfortable going around the managers and dealing directly with the front-line supervisors on certain issues that interested him.

Fido Gets Fed (the price paid for overloyalty)

Vince had to approve any writeoffs if an account was deemed uncollectible. One day he reviewed a report and saw a large balance due for a particular customer. He called Mario into his office and said, "Hey, I have an idea on what we could do with this one." Mario said, "Oh, that's already been resolved." Vince looked surprised and replied, "What do you mean, it's been resolved? It hasn't been written off yet." Mario started stammering, "Well . . . Ben had a suggestion that we should talk with the district sales office on that one." Vince quickly responded, "Oh Ben did, did he! Did you bump into him in the hallway and talk about it?" Mario furtively looked away and murmured, "Well, no . . . we had a meeting in his office." Vince said, "How long has this been going on?" Mario replied, "Mmm, since you've been in this job."

Vince was upset but quickly gathered his composure and said, "The next time Ben calls you, I want you to call me and come by my office and pick me up. I don't care if I'm in a meeting or on the phone. I don't care, in fact, if I'm under the desk drinking gin, for goodness sake. We will be going to Ben's office *together*." (Okay, he was kidding about the gin part.) Mario said, "Ben isn't going to like that," and Vince responded sharply, "Well, I don't like it either but this is what I need to do to be successful in this job."

Fido Gets Fired (action taken)

The next morning, Mario was at Vince's office door saying, "I just got the call from Ben." Vince sang out with his best Jackie Gleason imitation, "and awayyyyyyy we go!" As they reached Ben's office, Ben took one look at Mario, then glanced at Vince and said, "I just called Mario." Vince calmly stated, "I understand that but I believe you're going to review some of Mario's accounts. I'd like to go over them as well." Ben replied, "This really is just a couple of questions I have about Mario's accounts. When I need to talk to you about this, I'll call you."

Vince decided to put a stake in the ground. He said, "These accounts are my responsibility. You put me in this job. I need to know what's going on to do my job well. So it concerns me because it's my department and I have the responsibility for it. I'm not leaving."

Ben tried to pull rank to get out of this sticky situation and huffed, "I want you to leave my office right now!" Vince coolly replied, "I'm not going anywhere until we talk about these accounts." Ben was embarrassed since this tawdry little episode was happening in front of Mario. Ben quickly glanced over at Mario and said, "Would you please leave us alone for a few minutes?" Mario bolted like a Chihuahua with its tail on fire, eager to escape this boiling cauldron before it exploded.

Vince respectfully closed the door to provide some privacy, walked over and sat down in a chair next to Ben's desk. Ben thundered at him, "I want you to leave my office right now!" Vince responded in a calm and measured voice, "I'm not leaving. We're going to have a discussion right here and now about who is in charge of this area, and what I need to do my job."

Vince continued, "I need to understand how to run this department so that I can produce good results for you. Who is in charge of the day-to-day operations here - you or me? Because if it's you, then you don't need me. If it's me, however, I need you to teach me. These workarounds to Mario are going to stop <u>right now</u>. By doing these workarounds, you're basically saying I don't know what I'm doing. Doing workarounds with Mario doesn't make me any smarter or any better. It doesn't help me to help you. I can't do my job effectively and take full responsibility for my own performance if you continue to do this. Right now, *you* are in my way - you are my obstacle. You're either going to teach me how to collect or you're going to leave me alone and let me fail. It's one or the other - you choose. Or you can call Security and just have me walked out the door."

Ben actually picked up the phone and shouted, "Do you want me to call Security?" Vince calmly replied, "You just go ahead and do whatever you think is best." Vince knew that Ben wouldn't go through with his threat - it was just the last act of a desperate man. Ben couldn't argue the fact that Vince simply wanted to learn and effectively manage his own department. Vince's intentions were pure and he had Ben over a barrel.

Ben was completely flummoxed and realized the war was lost. He gave a long sigh. The irony was that Ben taught Vince how to do this - to confront in a healthy way, stand up for what he felt was right and deal with an issue as fast as possible. Now the monster that Ben created had come back to haunt him. Ben said softly, "Okay, I see your point but I can't have you doing things like this in front of the supervisors - you embarrassed me in front of Mario." Ben was looking for one last morsel to maintain his pride.

Vince would have none of that. He quickly cut off Ben and said, "I am <u>not</u> going to let you off the hook on this one.

You started this because *you* called in the supervisor who reports to me for a meeting, <u>not</u> because I called the supervisor. *You* embarrassed *me* in front of Mario." Ben sat there looking somewhat stunned, slowly composed himself and continued, "Okay, I see your point but I can't have you doing this in the office and making these kinds of statements." Vince responded, "Okay - as long as you don't do the workarounds with Mario, I won't make these kinds of statements." Ben said, "Right, it's a deal." They both stood up, calmly shook hands and smiled at each other. Good dogs! Ben never, ever called Mario into his office again without informing Vince - and Ben and Vince remained friends.

Paws To Reflect - Counterproductive Steps (key lessons)

Most people, unlike Vince, would have avoided healthy confrontation in this situation. Avoidance would have made it easier for the unacceptable, undermining behavior to continue - letting the offender know there would be little or no consequence. People teach others how to treat them by the way they allow themselves to be treated. Vince's confrontation with Ben, however, should not have occurred in front of other employees, if possible.

Paws To Reflect - Productive Steps (key lessons)

Vince realized that he had to confront Ben. He had no choice if he was going to continue to work in the department and enjoy performing his job to his fullest capability. Vince focused on what he *needed* from Ben - he didn't try to *fix* Ben. He brought the true issues to light and immediately clarified and dealt with the hidden agendas. Vince chose not to remain allegiant to an old belief of 'never confront your leader', since Ben had become his barrier. If Vince had simply put up with Ben, then he would have had only himself to blame.

Vince took a chance when he went into Ben's office and sat down in that chair. It was not an easy thing for him to do - it was a calculated risk. Vince, however, knew Ben very well. He had built a good relationship with Ben by laying the groundwork over a long period of time.

Vince knew with whom and what he was dealing. He played with fire but he understood the nature of the flame. He and Ben usually had a very good rapport and Vince knew what he could reasonably address. Vince knew Ben would not fire him and that Ben was just a blustery blowhard at times. Vince knew deep down that Ben had a good heart and was intelligent and secure enough to respond positively to the situation. Ben was a fair man and supported people he believed had pure intentions and whose hearts were in the right place.

Confronting is important in any good, healthy working relationship - it is an act of telling the truth as one perceives it. Caring enough to confront in an honest and healthy way is an act of true friendship. M. Scott Peck wrote, "There is a traditional concept that friendship should be a conflict-free relationship. . . . Such relationships are superficial and intimacy-avoiding. . . . Mutual loving confrontation is a significant part of all successful and meaningful human relationships. Without it the relationship is either unsuccessful or shallow." [21]

People aren't necessarily going to love each other while the confrontation is occurring. While this kind of heat caused sparks to fly in the moment, no mud was flung. It ultimately created enlightenment and awareness. Open and honest confrontation was good for the business and helped it run more effectively and productively in the long term.

People should address this type of undermining head on and right away. They should hold the offending party's feet to the fire. The secret to effective healthy confrontation is consistency - people should point out these undermining behaviors to the offender each time they occur.

An openly confrontational approach in the moment, as depicted in this chapter, is necessary on occasion. Not everyone is as bullheaded as Ben, however, so people should take that into account. Other situations may require a less dramatic approach. People should choose their battles smartly. There's no point in winning the battle if it means losing the war. It's not one size fits all!

Best Of Breed:
People teach others how to treat them
by the way they allow themselves to be treated.

When Your Fido Is...
Suffering From A Person
Who Drives You Crazy

But he who is joined with all the living has hope,
for a living dog is better than a dead lion.
-- The Bible, Ecclesiastes (9:4)

Bonnie was a Manager in the Accounting Department for WellAviation, a large company based in Minnesota that supplied aircraft parts to its customers. Bonnie reported for many years to Dennis, a Director in the area. Dennis was a micromanager - highly motivated by an intense drive to get things done, with an aggressive and single-minded focus.

Into The Doghouse (the trouble begins)

Dennis was extremely tough, demanding and judgmental with himself - as he was with others. When under pressure to produce results within very short timeframes, he reverted to the natural human trait of managing in an autocratic and controlling manner. Dennis constantly second-guessed Bonnie and worked her like a dog. His intentions were good - his desire to control was driven by wanting to obtain good outcomes. Control gave Dennis a sense of security that he knew what was going on all the time, and appeared to him to be the easiest and most effective way to get things done.

Dennis' staff perceived him as a fire-breathing dragon - a demeaning and frightening bully, in addition to being an annoying micromanager. He exhibited one of the most destructive underlying assumptions in business - 'that people will respond progressively better when they are treated progressively worse'.[22] During one meeting, Dennis yelled at Bonnie, telling her she hadn't done enough on her project and made him look bad to his peers. His constant second-guessing of Bonnie's every step, of course, drove her crazy and caused her to take an overly cautious approach on the project. She clammed up and felt ashamed and inferior. Bonnie simply couldn't stand being around Dennis any longer. Even thoughts of doing him bodily harm seemed somewhat satisfying!

Fido Gets Fed (the price paid for overloyalty)

Bonnie felt powerless to deal with Dennis' demanding management style. She always responded to each of her leaders exactly the same way and didn't see any options other than simply coping with Dennis. Bonnie's allegiance to the status quo left her stuck, timid and completely stressed out. She developed stress-related physical ailments and sought medical care.

Fido Gets Fired (action taken)

Bonnie decided, finally, to work with a career counselor to help her deal with this issue. Together they developed an effective approach to manage Dennis. She documented the major items that were truly important to her as far as being respected - what she *needed* and felt. She described in very *specific* detail what each of these items meant to her and what they looked like in terms of both Dennis' appropriate and inappropriate behavior. Bonnie described a very clear picture of what she needed him to do. One of the items stated, "Respect to me means you will not raise your voice - either directed at me or at anyone in my presence. My hearing is perfect and I need you to speak in a normal tone of voice. If you yell, I will get up and say, 'When you are ready to talk about this in a normal tone of voice, then I will return. Gotta go now'. I will then <u>leave</u> the room."

Bonnie sent a copy of this document to Dennis, along with her regular monthly report, prior to their next monthly one-to-one meeting. Nobody ever had the courage to stand up to him like this before. She was nervous and feared the situation would become very uncomfortable and he might blow up. The day came for Bonnie's meeting with Dennis. The moment of truth had arrived - there was no turning back. As she walked toward the meeting room, she felt trepidation and her palms began sweating. She thought to herself, "Oh my goodness, what am I doing? Why am I confronting this guy? He's a tank who can roll right over me!" She calmed down a bit using a quick meditation technique and steeled herself for the impending confrontation.

Bonnie entered Dennis' office and sat down. He didn't bother with any pleasantries and started asking her questions about the status of her latest project. After his queries were resolved, Bonnie said she wanted to review the document she had sent him prior to the meeting. Dennis admitted he hadn't read it and asked her to proceed. She pulled out two copies and gave one to him. Bonnie read out loud, in a positive and respectful manner, the entire list of what respect meant to her. She described how the things Dennis said and did affected her job effectiveness and their working relationship.

Dennis was completely shocked. He visibly winced as she described his past behaviors, point by point. He exclaimed, "I never did those things!" Bonnie replied, "Yes, you did but you just don't remember doing them." Dennis grudgingly motioned for her to continue. She described exactly *how* she needed to be treated in the future. He didn't realize his actions had been so inappropriate and the negative impact they were having on Bonnie. Dennis asked if he could have some time to think over her request and if they could meet again in a few weeks. She agreed. The blowup she had feared never occurred.

Bonnie and Dennis met again a few weeks later and discussed her request. He agreed to try to follow each item on the list. He never yelled at her again and she never had to reinforce the agreement by having to remind him. The approach stopped him dead in his tracks. The healthy confrontation worked! Dennis appreciated the information because it gave him a roadmap to Bonnie's emotions. He was not evil. He didn't get up out of bed each morning thinking, "Gee, how can I try to make Bonnie's life miserable today?" He just acted on instinct.

Bonnie discovered that if Dennis simply 'knew better', then he would 'do better'. In one fell swoop, they developed a way to work together more effectively. She found that she never had to create a huge emotional scene. Most people avoid healthy confrontation because they think it's going to blow up into a big yelling match, with people storming out of the office and slamming doors. For many years, Bonnie underestimated the ability of people (even overbearing people) to be able to respond to this kind of healthy feedback approach.

Paws To Reflect - Counterproductive Steps (key lessons)

Most people, unlike Bonnie, are not willing to make the difficult decisions and confront in a healthy way when necessary. Their unwillingness to experience short-term discomfort causes long-term pain and suffering. Short-term discomfort may be unavoidable but suffering is optional. Many people cope endlessly with an unhappy or unhealthy situation, hoping against hope that the other person will change.

Paws To Reflect - Productive Steps (key lessons)

Bonnie moved outside her comfort zone by communicating her perception of the truth appropriately and clearly to the person with whom she felt most uncomfortable. She retrieved her own power and took responsibility for her part of the communication. She planned out a very thorough approach to confronting Dennis in a healthy way. Bonnie learned the value of consistent boundary setting, not being intimidated and taking care of herself. Rather than trying to understand the motivation behind Dennis' behavior, she focused on what she *needed* - communicating her expectations to the person who needed to know. She didn't try to defend or justify how she felt in order to convince him, since that would have just added to the intensity of the situation. By giving him the detailed tools, Bonnie taught Dennis exactly how to treat her. It wasn't enough for her to simply say, "Dennis, please treat me with respect."

Planning ahead and learning to stay calm in intense situations is important. People who feel uncomfortable about confronting someone for the first time should write out what they want to say ahead of time - word for word if necessary. They can share it in confidence with a trusted friend or professional advisor to obtain feedback and practice what they plan to say, how they will say it and how to react to a few possible scenarios from the person being confronted. This method increases both a person's confidence and competence in the healthy confrontation approach. Although not necessary, it may be a good idea to take the document into the room during the actual confrontation. Reading it word for word to the person being confronted is better than not being prepared and reacting poorly if a blowup occurs. Harriet Lerner wrote, "Toning down our reactivity is perhaps the most crucial and difficult step . . . toward solving any human problem." [23]

Bonnie didn't confuse standing up for herself with trying to change Dennis. She gave him a chance to prove he could treat her respectfully and then had to let go of the result. She couldn't have any expectation that he would change his behavior. All Bonnie could do was observe his reaction and see if he was willing to work with her. How Dennis reacted was up to him - that was his responsibility and not any reflection upon her. If he hadn't responded well to her efforts and continued to blow up, then her choices would have been much more clear and informed. If she consciously chose to stay and report to him, then she would have given up her right to complain about her situation. If Bonnie chose to leave, then she had a very valid reason to do so. If she never tried this particular approach, however, then she didn't really have enough information to make her decision. In the end, she wasn't forced to leave the area.

Bonnie felt much better about remaining in a place where she could succeed and have more F.U.N. doing her job. Her ability to manage stress was greatly helped by her improved flexible problem solving skills and she no longer required a doctor's care. Bonnie's problem was a lot less difficult to solve than she had imagined. Not only did this new approach help her in the workplace but it was a great approach for other life situations as well. Ten minutes of discomfort resolved *years* of chronic pain and misery.

Best Of Breed:
If people wait for someone else to change first,
then they could be waiting for a <u>very</u> long time.
People, however, <u>can</u> teach an old dog new tricks,
such as 'what respect means to them'.

When Your Fido Is...
Sticking With A Corporate Cult Leader

Cry "Havoc!" and let slip the dogs of war.
                                    -- William Shakespeare, *Julius Caesar*

Brian was a Project Manager in the Investment Department of the Illinois division of LynchAndBull, a large firm based in New York. The company provided financial services to its business and consumer clients.

Brian had a strong desire to succeed and was very frustrated it took the company an average of 18 months to launch a new product to market. Since time was the primary currency of the new millennium, a new department was created to develop strategic technical systems to bring new products to market in as few as four months.

Carol, the Vice President of this new department, recruited Brian by wooing him with the chant, "Come, be a part of this chosen and elite special mission. Blaze new trails and pioneer exciting new systems. Together we will show the rest of the company how it can really be done." Brian didn't realize that Carol was actually one of the Sirens from Homer's epic poem *The Odyssey*, trying to entice him into crashing his life onto the rocks for her sake. Like Odysseus' men, he should have stopped up his ears with wax while he still had the chance to steer his own life away from danger! Brian was unconsciously drawn, alas, like a moth to the flame. He accepted the new position and moved from Illinois to New York - his hand caught in the leash of the hound bound for hell.

Into The Doghouse...Of Hell (the trouble begins)
Brian quickly found himself involved in a cult-like project - certainly not a murderous cult such as Jim Jones and the People's Temple - but a project that exhibited cultish tendencies. The main clues were: 1) it was countercultural and revolutionary, 2) it was personality-based, 3) the regular rules didn't apply and 4) there was a strong emphasis on keeping secrets. A brief description of each characteristic follows:
Countercultural and revolutionary: In a cult project, the abnormal becomes normal. Approaches the rest of the company views as unacceptable are considered standard operating procedure. All systems development in the firm followed a long, drawn-out, step-by-step procedure. Many people were more concerned with following processes 'to a T' than in speedy project completion. Carol made no attempt to hide her disdain for the company's approved systems development approaches. Her approach took incredibly complex concepts and developed them in parallel with each other. She was smart enough to pull it off but it ran completely contrary to the existing culture and how the company developed systems.
Personality-based: The entire project was embodied in Carol, the inventor and evangelist. She developed the concept and strategic vision to create more flexible systems to meet extremely aggressive product introduction timeframes. Carol was a master at using persuasion, emotional intimidation and peer pressure to make people feel guilty if they didn't follow her. She exuded a contentious attitude that implied she knew what she was doing while the rest of the firm was populated with boneheads and foot-draggers.

Regular rules didn't apply: A cult project operates as if many existing company rules and processes simply don't apply because 'we're different'. As mentioned, Carol openly ignored the mandated systems development methodology and showed little regard for how the rest of the company operated. Instead of proactively designing a compromise solution to maintain the spirit of the methodology, she steadfastly defied it.   She even publicly antagonized the company's Chief Information Officer over this issue.

Keeping Secrets: Carol managed in a fear-based way and kept a veil of secrecy over the project. Team members were told to be extremely careful when giving information to people 'outside the family', because 'they would not know how to handle the information'. It was clearly an 'us vs. them' orientation. Anyone who communicated regularly with people outside the core team was viewed as a possible spy and people who left the team were often denounced as traitors.

The Hound From Hell Gets Fed (the price paid for overloyalty)
Brian and Carol got along well, in general, and often went to lunch together with their work team. Brian had committed his heart and soul to the project and worked countless 14 hour days with very little time off. He had very limited time, unfortunately, to develop any hobbies or personal relationships outside of work while living in a new city. He was frustrated and burned out, which had a palpable impact on his overall quality of life. This wasn't helped by what he perceived as Carol's often abusive leadership approach.

One encounter (out of countless examples) typified the leadership style Carol exhibited when dealing with most people. It occurred during a business trip she and Brian took to visit with their software development team located in Philadelphia.

Brian had met earlier that day with the Marketing department. Carol had met with him prior to that meeting, since she wasn't going to be able to attend, and told him not to give Marketing any specific dates concerning project status or completion. Although his regular mode of operation was to communicate project information openly to project constituents, Brian did *exactly* as he was instructed. Later that evening, Brian and Carol were on the same train from New York to Philadelphia. They happened to be sitting, by chance, in separate sections of the train. Upon arrival, Brian departed the train and waited for Carol, while hundreds of people milled around the station. He was not prepared for what was about to occur.

Carol stormed off the train, looked Brian straight in the eye, pointed her bony finger in his face and screamed, "I CAN'T BELIEVE YOU SAID WHAT YOU SAID TODAY IN THAT MEETING!" She then launched into a scathing diatribe. Carol heard from someone else, apparently, that Brian took an action during the meeting she felt compromised the project. Brian's face turned red - he was livid that he was being attacked unfairly and felt a huge amount of embarrassment it was being done in such a public setting. He felt violated.

The next day Brian thought about what had occurred. He understood the cost to him of remaining in a bad situation. He had a choice - to act in his own best interest or simply gripe about his situation. Griping would have left him feeling powerless and hopeless. Brian realized that could undermine his energy as well as short-circuit his ability to contribute to the fullest extent possible. He decided to act to protect himself from the ravages of the overpowering cult leader.

The Hound From Hell Gets Fired (action taken)

The first thing Brian realized was that he was not going to change Carol. He needed to accept her and just let mad dogs lie - she was who she was. She sincerely believed she was on a heroic quest and that her leadership techniques helped the project move toward a successful completion. Carol wasn't trying to jeopardize the project. She felt the end justified her means and the many casualties strewn in her wake were simply the price to be paid.

Brian stopped taking her insults so personally. He realized Carol's abusive behaviors were just her dysfunctional people management techniques. Brian focused on simply trying to achieve the specific results that kept Carol off his back. He started leaving the office by 6:00 P.M. each workday and attempted to create a more balanced life outside work.

Brian also realized that regardless of how well-intentioned the cult project, it had the built-in disease of 'short-term-itis'. By definition, Carol's team was a small, highly-focused group that pursued new ideas outside the mainstream organization. Her group would be swallowed up eventually by the larger organization. Its lifespan would be generally two to three years. Brian focused his attention on aligning with the larger organization, especially to areas he might want to move to *when* (not if) the cult project imploded. Using military metaphors, he: 1) developed his air cover, 2) protected his flanks and 3) ensured his ground support. A brief description of each strategy follows:

Air Cover: Brian developed his air cover with senior management - especially from groups outside the cult organization. He built coalitions with numerous members of senior management, both within his direct line of hierarchy above Carol as well as in the organization as a whole. He met with members of senior management to make sure they were aware of his contributions toward overall company goals. Brian communicated his role and worth and developed his reputation within the wider organization. Most importantly, he made sure he maintained grudging respect for Carol herself.

Even though he didn't always like her, he continued to respect her immense strategic and tactical business abilities. They maintained a workable truce. Brian did his job well and gave Carol no reason to complain about his performance.

Flank Protection: Brian protected his flanks - the lateral relationships he developed with peers and colleagues. He became closely aligned with his two peers reporting to Carol and developed a climate of mutual respect. They made numerous deposits into the 'trust banks' of one another. Brian also connected with his peers in the larger organization seeking out opportunities to export his strategic systems experience onto platforms for greater customer impact within the company.

Ground Support: Brian always did an effective job cultivating ground support at the employee level. He engendered the undying respect and loyalty of the team that reported to him. He realized any animosity at the ground support level would doom him. Brian ensured his indispensability to the team by playing a very important role in its ongoing performance. He constantly coached and taught them, and they operated as a true unit. He also organized softball games, periodic accomplishment celebration dinners and day-to-day recognition of the team's efforts.

Brian's networking paid off within a short time. After successfully completing the initial implementation phase of the project, he sought and accepted another position within the company.

Paws To Reflect - Counterproductive Steps (key lessons)

Brian understood that an organization needs 'corporate mavericks' such as Carol to challenge the limits and move the company to higher levels of achievement. Carol's strategies were brilliant but the way she handled people was abysmal. Whether she had her facts straight about Brian's actions at the

Marketing meeting wasn't the issue. What mattered was *how* she delivered the information. Although she thought her facts were correct, in reality her facts were incorrect. Brian hadn't done any of the things she accused him of doing.

The relationship between Carol and Brian was never the same again. While Brian remained professional and did enough to meet his job requirements, his passion was no longer there. Whatever Carol thought she was accomplishing with her attack was not worth the price she paid. She lost his heart and his long-term tenure in the department.

Brian prepared to move to his new job within the company. He would work two weeks in his present job, ordinarily, before moving to the new job. Carol asked him, as a personal favor to her, to extend this time to six weeks for the good of the project. *In spite of* the way he had been treated by her in the past, he agreed. Carol then left the company for another job before Brian's six week period was completed! He felt manipulated.

Brian fell into a pattern common to people who have been mistreated over a long period of time in a negative work environment. It's the corporate version of the 'Stockholm Syndrome'. This phenomenon describes hijacked or kidnapped prisoners who wind up sympathizing and bonding with their captors. They believe obedience to their captor's demands will make everything turn out fine. One famous 1970s example of this syndrome was Patty Hearst and the Symbionese Liberation Army cult.

Cult leaders constantly wear people down and treat them in a way that slowly erodes their self-esteem. The way people are treated soon becomes the way they think they deserve to be treated. Many people wind up perceiving themselves the way the cult leader perceives them. They feel like hostages to the situation and stick with it no matter the cost. They tell themselves they can't leave due to their financial commitments or security concerns (see chapter *When Your Fido Is...Fixating On Security*). The real reason many people don't escape, in fact, is due to the corporate Stockholm Syndrome.

Paws To Reflect - Productive Steps (key lessons)

Brian, luckily, only had a mild case of the syndrome. Rather than feeling like a captive in New York, he took personal responsibility for his career and didn't wait for the company to take care of him.

What Brian didn't do, for example, was just as important as what he did. He didn't try to change Carol - he focused on changing himself. He understood he always should be working *on* his career rather than just *in* his career. Brian's allegiance to his own needs and how he needed to be treated allowed him to move on to a more enjoyable role within the company. His situation didn't require an actual confrontation with Carol - it was about Brian confronting issues within himself.

Brian learned the hard way that when a cult leader asks him to jump on the train, he'd better watch out. He found out that may be the last whistle stop on the one-way trip to the devil's doghouse!

Best Of Breed:

Trying to change someone else is like expecting a Chihuahua to protect a person from being attacked in a bad part of town.
Rule #1: Learn how to protect oneself.
Rule #2: Stay away from bad parts of town.

CAUTIONARY TAILS
How To Deal With Lovable But Underperforming People

> So far in *Firing Fido!*, the primary focus has been on dealing with all the behavior obstacles (Fidos) inside people, whether they were Caged Fidos that people <u>fully</u> controlled (e.g., the company where they chose to work) or Uncaged Fidos people <u>partially</u> controlled (e.g., who their leader was). The only things people truly control, of course, are their own thoughts and behaviors.
>
> Let's shift our attention now to dealing with external folks - those lovable but often underperforming people who become a big obstacle to a team's success.

Do You Know A Person Named *Scooby-Doo*?

Rikes!

-- Scooby-Doo

One of the biggest mistakes people can make is hiring their best friends. Although well-meaning and endearing, a best friend can quickly turn into a worst enemy. Some of the trickiness of dealing with friends was already referenced in the previous chapters:

- *When Your Fido Is...Overattachment To Family Beliefs*
- *When Your Fido Is...Juggling A Family Business And Ethics*
- *When Your Fido Is...Overidentifying With The 'Gang' Or Team*

Scooby-Doo is a cartoon example of an endearing and well-intentioned dog who was a constant source of frustration. The gangly and lovable pup spent much of his time hunting for chocolate and eating whatever he could lay his greedy paws on. He was always ready and willing for an adventure, although he was often nervous and whimpered loudly. Shaggy and the rest of the 'gang' of teenage sleuths, of course, adored Scooby in spite of his warts. They had fun when Scooby got excited at the prospect of receiving his delightful Scooby Snack and saluted them while barking, "Scooby-Dooby-Dooooooooo!"

Scooby often infuriated the gang with his clowning - chasing other dogs, hiding in planters or knocking off peoples' glasses by mistake. Scooby's near-catastrophes usually delayed the ultimate resolution of the mystery the sleuths were investigating. Scooby discovered clues or caught the villain many times, often in spite of himself, by mistakenly falling on him or literally tripping over a major clue. Although Scooby's buffoonery *eventually* solved the mystery or uncovered the plot, he was a high-maintenance member of the team . . . just like many employees. The unintended havoc many employees create can often be a headache to endure.

Let's take a look at how the behaviors of a particular Scooby affected TotalRelations, a small firm in California. The company provided marketing and public relations services to its clients as well as customized website development.

Jack, the President of the startup company, hired his best friend Harry to be Vice President in charge of Web Development. Jack ran the marketing and public relations side of the business while Harry was in charge of website development.

Jack and Harry were friends since childhood and had been through a lot together. They took numerous vacations together with their wives. Both of their families worked at the company and some of their family members even dated one another. Jack often said to his employees, "I look at this business as a family - we look out for each other and we take care of each other." He didn't realize, however, that Harry, as an employee, was the working definition of a Scooby.

Into The Doghouse (the trouble begins)

Harry was responsible for bringing in a steady stream of corporate clients but he did not fulfill his commitments. He acted more like a Web development contractor than the Vice President of Web Development. Harry promised, month after month (and year after year!) that certain accounts were going to lead to increased sales volume. It never happened. Harry built websites for one client and then moved on to the next client for the next job. He was not motivated to cultivate and leverage relationships or expand services within an existing client. Harry never proactively developed any company business strategy. He waited for Jack to do the complex thinking for him and then simply followed. Rather than being a regular Scooby who *eventually* got the job done in spite of himself, Harry *never* met the requirements for his job as a Vice President. He became a truly destructive version of a Scooby.

Jack tried desperately to avoid constructive confrontation concerning Harry's performance, even though the evidence was overwhelming. Jack avoided dealing with <u>any</u> issues concerning Harry's behaviors. He trained Harry how to treat him by not enforcing agreements, not evaluating performance on an ongoing basis and not providing consequences.

Jack complained about Harry to others but never directly confronted Harry with the truth as he perceived it. Jack wasn't being fair to Harry and he wasn't building mutual trust. Harry was a master at confusion and delay tactics. Whenever Jack even came close to broaching the topic of Harry's performance, Harry simply changed the subject.

The confrontation avoidance at the firm brings to mind the scene from the 1999 dark comedy film *Office Space* where the 'Two Bobs' (efficiency consultants) are meeting with Initech company management. They are discussing the potential layoff of various employees and the fate of one underperforming employee, Milton, in particular. The first Bob says, "We can't actually find a record of him being a current employee . . . apparently what happened is that he was laid off five years ago and no one ever told him about it. But through some kind of glitch in the payroll department, he still gets a paycheck . . . so we just went ahead and fixed the glitch." Initech's Division Vice President responds, "Mmmm, great . . . so Milton has been let go?" The other Bob says, "Well, no . . . we fixed the glitch. Milton won't be receiving a paycheck anymore . . . so it'll just work itself out naturally. We always like to avoid confrontation whenever possible. Problem solved from your end." They were hoping that Milton would just figure it out and leave on his own - no muss, no fuss. With its similar avoidance of any confrontation, Jack's company might as well have been called Initech <u>Junior</u>!

Jack found himself in the position of unconsciously taking care of Harry, which led to all sorts of negative business results. Similar to the situation referenced in the chapter *When Your Fido Is...Overattachment To Family Beliefs*, Jack made excuses to others under the guise of *caring*, which made Harry more ineffectual over time.

The bulk of the company's business, for many years, came from the marketing and public relations side rather than the Web development side. The firm's overall success covered up for Harry's lack of performance. An economic downturn, however, caused the marketing and public relations revenues to shrivel. This exposed Harry's lack of performance.

Jack finally had to do something. To refocus his business and target his marketing investments in a more cost-effective manner, Jack decided to concentrate the organization's entire marketing efforts on the health care industry. As a small business, he knew he couldn't afford to market to everyone. He felt the company had the most experience in, and was best at servicing, that particular market niche. While he continued to accept any type of business that came in the door, the company's marketing efforts were directed at health care companies. Jack also set performance targets for every member of the firm.

Harry, unfortunately, had very little experience with the health care industry, since most of his Web development contacts were with other industries. He freaked out and fought the decision vociferously. He had a nice place to go to work and do all the things he wanted. Suddenly, the situation had changed. Now there would be accountability, measurement of results and sales goals. "Aaaarrrggghhh!" Harry silently screamed to himself.

Harry, in reality, wasn't the person Jack thought he hired in the first place. Harry was *never* capable of performing the job of Vice President of Web Development. It did not become an issue, however, until the economic downturn forced the firm to get its act together and focus for the first time since its inception.

Jack finally confronted Harry but used an overly aggressive approach. Jack tried to convince Harry to accept the changes by describing in detail the dire position the organization found itself in. He threatened Harry with a get-on-board-or-get-off-the-train speech. All that did was increase Harry's defensiveness. Harry felt embarrassed that he had received this free ride for so long. He was now put into a position where he had, "some splainin' to do," as Ricky Ricardo often said on *I Love Lucy*. Harry, however, couldn't explain and justify the situation. He became very angry and frustrated and lashed out at Jack. Harry's anger, of course, was simply a coverup to avoid having to reveal his embarrassment. He was a tough customer and saw an opportunity to cover his own rear end and maintain his pride.

Fido Gets Fed (the price paid for overloyalty)

Harry sued Jack for breach of contract and defamation of character. Harry argued he never agreed to perform only health care Web development. He also accused Jack of badmouthing him to other firms in the area and sabotaging efforts to get his own Web development business up and running.

The situation was truly uncomfortable, since both Jack and Harry belonged to the same professional accreditation organization and had many of the same contacts. Ironically, the friendship and emotional energy they felt toward each other coming into the business actually contributed to their eventual level of animosity. There was more energy to deal with when things started going south. A thin line often separates love and hate and that sense of betrayal wounded them both.

Jack, incredibly, *continued* to let Harry do his Web development work on behalf of the company rather than severing business relations immediately after being served with the lawsuit. Jack's overloyalty to Harry just made the situation worse - an elongated ordeal that was unbearable for everyone.

Harry was allowed to hang on for so long that the damage to the organization was overwhelming. The firm divided into a pro-Scooby coalition and an anti-Scooby coalition. Some people, ultimately, rallied to Harry's cause and felt sorry for him, simply because he was the underdog. People said, "Look at what they're doing to poor Harry - they're hounding him out of the company. They're kicking him when he's down. How unfair!" Even though the damage to the firm was clear and their own livelihoods were jeopardized, many people still became overly sentimental.

The members of the 'Harry coalition' slowed their work whenever Jack asked them to do something. People loyal to Jack, likewise, did the same for Harry's requests. This caused an enormous amount of work to be picked up by each of the opposing camps trying to get tasks accomplished. The unhealthy conflict thwarted the morale of everyone working in the company. It caused an incredible price to be paid by the employees, by the customers and by the shareholders of the organization.

Firing Fido!

Fido Finally Gets Fired (action taken)

The lawsuit between Jack and Harry was eventually settled out of court and Harry left to start his own firm. The entire episode, sadly, caused Jack a lot of pain, aggravation and financial loss.

Paws To Reflect - Counterproductive Steps (key lessons)

Jack avoided acting early and quickly to confront Harry's performance issues in a healthy way. As the old *Fram* oil filter commercial said, "You can pay me now or you can pay me later!" Jack was going to pay, in any case, for his mistake in hiring Harry. The cost would have been *far* less if he had addressed the issue promptly rather than allowing a situation to develop that resulted in a lawsuit.

Jack's first mistake was to base his initial hiring decision on his friendship with Harry. He did not review a roster of candidates and assess performance and qualifications in an objective manner. Jack's judgment of Harry's performance was clouded by his friendship and this created a blind spot.

Jack made the *Fatal Fido* error of leadership - he was more concerned with being liked first and respected second. Friends know all about each other, warts and all - they like and accept one another just the way they are. They find their differences, in fact, somewhat endearing - that's probably why they're friends in the first place. Because they know, like and trust each other, they believe they will *also* work well together. Major mistakey, Jakey. These endearing differences can be deadly to a business partnership. Peoples' true selves are revealed in a business situation - especially their relationship to power, control and money.

Work relationships are based on hierarchy - one person reporting to another - while friend relationships are based on equality. Friend relationships don't work well in a hierarchy.

When people play more than one role in each other's lives (e.g., both friend and leader), that situation is usually fraught with difficulty. This is due to the conflicting role expectations. The path of friends who try to work together in a business is littered with broken relationships. Jack avoided healthy confrontation, unfortunately, which subsequently caused the blowup to occur.

Jack didn't act in the best interest of his organization because he looked at it as a family first and a business second. That's a bad arrangement for long-term business success - a rabid dog for sure! As described in the chapter *When Your Fido Is...Juggling A Family Business And Ethics*, anytime the family structure is more important than the business structure, the company is on the way to becoming a dead dog.

Paws To Reflect - Productive Steps (key lessons)

Many people have the greatest difficulty dealing openly and honestly with the people closest to them - it's easier to fire a stranger than it is to fire a best friend. A leader must be willing to fire Fido, or Fido will get him fired eventually. The best way, of course, for a leader to avoid this problem in the first place is to <u>not</u> hire his best friend!

Firing Harry for non-performance much earlier in the game would have been good business strategy. It would have been doing right by the business and providing superior returns to the shareholders. While it's never comfortable to fire someone such as Harry, it is fair. Confronting the performance issue and taking action is fair to the business, it's fair to the customers, it's fair to the leaders and it's fair to the team. Most importantly, it's fair to Harry himself - it's not scheming or unethical in any way. Firing someone when it's justified is actually the principled thing to do. *To tell the truth as one perceives it in an appropriate manner is the highest and purest form of respect.* The gift of honesty is the most precious gift a leader can give another person.

Deep down, at some level, it's actually a relief to people such as Harry to be let go. They have been struggling to do a job they simply cannot do - they are distraught and in pain. They certainly aren't having any F.U.N.! Most of the time, people like Harry are frustrated and actually want to leave but can't bring themselves to do it. The caring leader actually helps people such as Harry to do what they can't do for themselves. As long as the separation is handled in a professional and respectful manner, people like Harry will tend to take it much better than anticipated . . . there's rarely a massive blowup. Rather than being the worst thing done to people such as Harry, being fired is often the best and most caring thing anyone ever did for them.

Best Of Breed:
*The majority of obstacles flow from
the inability to deal appropriately and <u>early</u>
with the 'people' issues.
"Fire Fido Or Fido Will Fire You!"*

CHRIS KOZAKIS

A TAIL OF A FATEFUL TRIP

Another familiar example of the bumbling and underperforming best friend such as *Scooby-Doo* is the lead character of the classic 1960s TV sitcom who drove everyone crazy. That's right, Gilligan of *Gilligan's Island*, one of the most delightful, stupefying and banal bits of fluff ever to soothe the brain. Gilligan was an endearing but incompetent bumbler. Although he was well-intentioned, his constant screwups were extremely damaging to the castaways' efforts to get off the uncharted desert island. Gilligan was the weakest link. Most telling of all, he was the Skipper's 'li'l buddy'. All the castaways became very comfortable and familiar with him - he was just so nice and likable. No one wanted to hurt his feelings, so they took care of him and shielded him from taking on too much responsibility. They accommodated and compensated for him with numerous workarounds. They treated him, in many ways, as a totally helpless and dependent child rather than as an adult.

Gilligan was more trouble than he was worth. He was, in fact, the sole reason all the castaways were still stuck on that island! The Professor went through an incredible amount of effort to come up with a series of ingenious inventions to allow them to get off the island. Then inept little Gilligan consistently destroyed the contraptions. The other castaways tried in vain to repair whatever he sabotaged but the gadgets never worked correctly again. Gilligan had horrible performance execution skills and wasn't doing anyone any good. He never seemed to learn from his experience. He was also in complete denial that he was the problem. He simply couldn't and wouldn't do the job. It didn't matter how much coaching or help Gilligan received from the others - he was unqualified and in over his head. It clearly wasn't in anyone's best interest to keep him around.

To paraphrase comedian Dennis Miller, 'The best description for solving a problem is to **KILL GILLIGAN** and get the hell off the island!' The Professor would have pieced together one last contraption, Gilligan wouldn't be around any longer to break it and they all would have been off the island within a week. Problem solved. The Professor could have taught the other castaways how to build rafts, how to navigate by the stars and various survival techniques - but none of it mattered until they removed the ultimate obstacle - Gilligan. (By *kill*, of course, I mean *remove*!)

The shipwrecked castaways overcomplicated the process - the answer was right in front of their noses the entire time. They created their dilemma by losing sight of their ultimate goal. The goal was not to make life more comfortable while on the island - the goal was to get off the damn island! Even the words of the *Gilligan's Island* theme song at the end of each show were a dead giveaway - 'to make them comfortable in their tropic island nest'. The castaways weren't trying to solve anything. They were just trying to make the situation as comfortable as possible.

So why was Gilligan the most difficult one to *kill*? . . . because everyone on the island was connected emotionally to him. He was so lovable - their 'li'l buddy'. The majority of all the obstacles - the Fidos - in most peoples' lives flow from their inability to deal appropriately with the 'Gilligan person'.

None of the castaways intentionally tried to make things so difficult. It's amazing what happens to good people who are stuck in a bad system. To paraphrase Peter Drucker, 'There is no greater waste of time than doing something better that should not be done at all'. The castaways coped for so long by putting up with and making the best of a bad situation that they got used to it. They worked very hard at trying to get off the island but confused accomplishing numerous tasks with making true progress. They focused on the process rather than the goal.

The castaways worked twice as hard as necessary, in fact, to avoid dealing with the core issue - to confront and remove Gilligan. They protected a togetherness tradition of 'all for one and one for all' - seven people were on the island and seven people had to get off the island together. It became more important for them to stay together as a group than it did for them to get off the island. The castaways made the mistake of believing they were somehow responsible for taking care of Gilligan - to manage, protect and compensate for him. By treating Gilligan as if he were a permanent fixture they had to put up with, Gilligan had all the true power within the group.

The castaways didn't take care of themselves or solve the real problem. The alternative to *killing* Gilligan was to stay potentially isolated and marooned on the desert island forever! As in most business situations, the castaways actually chose to stay on the island forever rather than deal directly with Gilligan. That was the price they were willing to pay. They sacrificed their own needs for the interests of the group. I'm not advocating *killing* people, of course, but some people should be removed from their positions or fired from the company.

Making something difficult is easy to do. As described in the TotalRelations story earlier in this chapter, Jack made things difficult by simply ignoring the situation and not addressing the root cause - Harry's lack of performance. Complexity naturally ensued because Jack avoided acting early and quickly to remove the Gilligan. Layer upon layer of agendas and unhealthy conflicts resulted. If a situation is overly complex, then that means the difficult choices haven't been made - people have accommodated rather than confronted. Look at the name of the classic TV sitcom . . . it was not called *The Professor's Island*, *The Skipper's Island* or

Ginger's Island. It <u>was</u> *Gilligan's Island* - defined by and revolving around the bumbler. TotalRelations might as well have been called *Harry's Island*!!! In business, a team's entire effort can revolve around trying to determine how to manage, cope and contend with the Gilligan. **Instead of managing the organization and serving its customers, the focus shifts to managing the Gilligan**.

Most Gilligans in business are certainly not as completely incompetent as the classic TV character. They are more like 'Situational Gilligans'. They know their job, by and large, as long as the situation remains 'business as usual' - a regular, comfortable, day-to-day routine. Many Gilligans are fine until they are pushed - then they get overwhelmed and become destructive. If they are pressured to excel in an area in which they are uncomfortable and don't have much experience, then they appear incompetent. They hate being asked to do things differently - to think and act 'outside the box' - to change, stretch or improve. Tension rises and they start to stumble.

Situational Gilligans mean well but many times will resist in a passive-aggressive manner. They won't follow up and move requests forward in a timely manner. They refer to their tasks as organizing '*your* meeting' and working on '*your* project'. Situational Gilligans hope against hope that the person pushing them will just go away and things will return to the way they used to be. It's all unconscious. They almost never consciously think, "How can I resist and actively sabotage the situation?"

Harry was actually a Situational Gilligan for many years at TotalRelations. He was able to provide website development in an effective manner - but nothing more. He was able to get the job done as long as the job didn't change. When things needed to be done differently, however, Harry fell apart and became a 'True Gilligan'. Even the classic TV character Gilligan was not trying to actively sabotage or get in the way. If the TV show had been set in Atlanta, then nobody would have needed to get off a deserted island. Gilligan would have been happy working some job at the local record store. As long as the boat didn't need to be rocked, Gilligan existed just fine and dandy. On the island, however, when people demanded something extra out of Gilligan, such as helping with the new gadget the Professor built, everything fell apart.

If an employee becomes a True Gilligan - adding minimal to no value while being clearly destructive - then he must be dealt with. This is a person who doesn't want to get it or is incapable of getting it. As *Gilligan's Island* proved, it took only <u>one</u> person to mess things up for everyone else. It will be the Gilligans that keep a wide variety of other people from doing what's in their own and the firm's best interest. Once these obstacles are removed, the remaining employees can become empowered, excited and more productive. They can focus on doing work they truly enjoy. **Healthy confrontation doesn't turn people off - it turns them on!**

While some employees are True Gilligans, others are more like *Scooby-Doos*. Like the cartoon dog, they are a headache to endure, cause numerous problems and delay the ultimate solutions. They do, however, tend to *eventually* come through and get the job done in spite of themselves. Here are some questions to ask concerning a Scooby situation:

- Do you have to follow up after Scooby and mend fences?
- Is the unintended havoc Scooby creates and the cost of putting up with him worth it?
- Are there others out there who could get the job done without all the drama of a high-maintenance Scooby?

The decision to *kill* Scooby is not as easy or clear as the decision to *kill* Gilligan but Scooby can make a situation overly complex.

ARE YOU FORCED TO PUT UP WITH
SOMEONE ELSE'S *SCOOBY-DOO* OR GILLIGAN?

A leader often makes the mistake of putting his own friends in place . . . the endearing people who swear their allegiance to him. A dog represents what many people value beyond anything else - loyalty - and people overlook <u>a lot</u> to get that. Whenever others in the company spot an underperforming person who is being protected by a friend, all they can do is shake their heads in dismay and murmur to themselves, "Ruh-roh!"

People are stuck putting up with this incompetent Scooby - picking up after, making excuses and covering up for him. It severely damages the morale of the entire team when the leader overlooks the resulting performance problems. Frustrated employees often suffer in silence and fantasize about the day when they will be able to finally sing with delight, "Scooby-Dooby-Doo . . . where are you? You're GONE from the com-pan-y now!"

It's rare for a 'protected Scooby' - an underperforming *pet* friend of your mutual leader - to be fired. What can conscientious employees do, given that reality, to protect themselves when stuck in these situations? Short-term discomfort may be unavoidable but suffering is optional. Suffering is doing other peoples' jobs in addition to your own and working to the exclusion of your personal life.

Since you can't change a protected Scooby (or, for that matter, a protected Gilligan), here are three things to help you deal with either:

1) Minimize, to the extent possible, the contact and interaction you have with Scooby, while ensuring the job still gets done.

2) Decide to set boundaries around the number of hours you'll work each day and clarify what you will and won't do.

- Simply enduring and picking up for others makes people feel resentful and angry. Anger clouds your clarity and judgment and gets in the way of understanding what you need.

3) Consistently reinforce appropriate boundaries with the inconsistent, scattered and disorganized Scooby who is making life miserable for you.

- When a Scooby forgets things or doesn't deliver on a promised task, don't pick up for him and cause yourself extra work. Remind him, instead, of his responsibilities in a professional manner. By doing this, you are teaching Scooby how you need to be treated. The reason most people don't confront him directly is due to their apprehension over his potentially negative emotional reaction to the request. It's really a choice between Scooby feeling badly or them feeling badly. Most people, actually, will choose to feel badly themselves rather than confront Scooby!

You should not, however, go to your mutual leader to complain about Scooby, unless there's an ethical or legal concern. One of the reasons Scooby is there in the first place is perhaps due to his friendship with the leader! This is a relationship issue that should be navigated directly between you and Scooby. If you require help, then discuss the situation in confidence with a trusted peer, friend or professional advisor. There are times when it may be best for conscientious employees to leave the project, department or company. At that point, of course, you should discuss the situation with your leader. If the situation is so unworkable it could torpedo careers, then leaving is always an option.

FIRING FIDO!

VARIOUS REASONS WHY IT'S DIFFICULT
TO FIRE A PERSON

Making the tough decision to confront a person is extraordinarily difficult for most people. It's foreign to how many of us were raised. We were brought up with messages such as 'don't rock the boat' and 'if you don't have something nice to say, then don't say anything at all'. As mentioned in the chapter *Caged And Uncaged Fidos*, most people were taught to cover up and make excuses for others under the guise of *caring*.

The reason confrontation is so difficult derives from our good intentions. People desire to be liked - we don't want to hurt others and we don't want to disappoint others or ourselves. Most of us *hate* having to tell people they have limitations that cannot be overcome in a particular situation. We also don't want to admit that we made a mistake in judgment by hiring our friend in the first place.

Emotional confrontation is one of the most difficult and challenging aspects of leadership. Even some of the Chief Executive Officers (CEOs) of the top Fortune 500 companies in the United States find this difficult. The authors of a recent *Fortune* magazine cover story performed a comprehensive study of several dozen major CEO failures during the 1990s, concluding:

"Most unsuccessful CEOs stumble because of one simple, fatal shortcoming. . . . So how do CEOs blow it? More than any other way, by failure to put the right people in the right jobs - and the related failure to fix people problems in time. Specifically, failed CEOs are often unable to deal with a few key subordinates whose sustained poor performance deeply harms the company . . . they usually know there's a problem; their inner voice is telling them, but they suppress it. . . . As one CEO says, 'It was staring me in the face, but I refused to see it'. The failure is one of emotional strength." [24]

Those extremely accomplished and articulate CEOs held positions of power at the highest levels of organizations and earned tens of millions of dollars a year. They had what it took to get to the top - the intelligence, vision and dedicated work ethic. Yet even *their* judgment blurred when they couldn't confront a key person's performance.

HOW TO FIRE A PERSON

Let's assume for a moment that a leader takes the high road with an underperforming employee. First, the leader scrupulously reviews his own behaviors and humbly deals with his own Caged and Uncaged Fidos to ensure he isn't doing anything to get in his own way or in other peoples' way.

Next, the leader tries very hard to work with the employee to improve performance. As early as possible, he calls attention to the employee's behaviors and explains the expected standards of performance with measurable goals. He then gives the employee an appropriate amount of time to change.

The leader holds the employee accountable for achieving the outcomes rather than trying to change his specific behaviors. The possible consequences of not meeting expectations are made clear. The leader follows up many times and carefully documents each performance improvement meeting. Each time, the leader reviews the mutually agreed-upon ideas, strategies and interim goals.

Communications are specific, constructive and to the point - treating the employee with dignity. The employee is treated as a person capable of change. The leader gives the employee positive and encouraging public feedback on a regular basis - 'catching him when he's doing it right'. The employee is given every reasonable chance to succeed.

Nothing works, however, or there is incremental improvement but not enough. The time comes to separate - to allow the employee the opportunity to try to prosper in another endeavor more appropriately suited to his abilities.   This doesn't necessarily mean, however, *firing* him from the company.

Problem resolution could be as simple as transferring him from a particular project in which he's not effective to another position within the organization. The employee may be better suited to a different role or a different area of the organization that better matches his strengths. This allows the employee to be an even better team player - executing to the best of his ability in the context of the team to which he belongs.

If an *actual* firing is being considered, however, the leader should observe the employee to determine if there are any signs of unstable behavior. Warnings include significant recent changes in dress, grooming, hygiene, irritability, overreactiveness or withdrawal. If any one of these behaviors is occurring, then a Human Resources representative should perform an assessment. It could reveal a recent divorce, loss of a relative/friend or a significant legal/financial problem.

A person's potential instability, of course, should be considered fully before any firing takes place. A company's termination procedure guidelines should also be adhered to in order to avoid litigation that can result from unfair dismissal cases.

In this case, we'll assume an actual firing is necessary, the employee is stable and the leader is in a decision-making position. The next page lists recommended steps to take to fire someone fairly, respectfully, professionally and quickly.

RECOMMENDED STEPS TO TAKE TO FIRE A PERSON

1) About 15 minutes prior to conducting the termination meeting, the leader should meet with any major constituents to inform them of his decision. At this point, he is not asking for their opinion or opening the situation up for discussion - he is simply giving them the courtesy of a 'heads-up'.

2) Conduct the termination meeting in a neutral office or conference room - not the leader's office and not the person's office.

3) Conduct the meeting with the person on a one-to-one basis. The most respectful way to treat him is to give the bad news face-to-face and not hand it off to a Human Resources representative.

4) Keep the meeting short, professional and direct. It's important to be fair and courteous, in order to preserve good, productive working relationships and avoid any bridge burning. The leader should be respectful and use well-chosen words - treating the person with professionalism.

5) Do not present this as an option - the leader is informing the person of his decision. The leader is not asking the person for a resignation - he is telling the person that he is being fired.

6) Say something such as, "This just isn't working out - we both know there are some limitations here. I think it would be best for all concerned if we part ways and move on. We'll cover you from a financial standpoint (severance, benefits, etc.) and provide for a job placement service for a period of time." [If the company normally offers this benefit.]

7) If the leader thinks it's appropriate, he may want to offer to use his own professional network to help the person find a new job.

8) Do not apologize for the decision that has been made.

9) Do not overdo attempts at trying to make the person feel better about the situation.

10) Do not suggest anything the person should do differently to improve his performance. The problem has been solved - the attempts to *fix* the person should stop.

11) Hand the employee the legal separation agreement without expecting him to sign it right away. He may choose to sign it. It's his prerogative, however, to review the agreement with an attorney.

12) Schedule the entire meeting to last no longer than 15-20 minutes. At the conclusion, the leader and the person shake hands and leave.

THE FINAL TAIL

Struggling With The Main Fido In My Life

When a dog bites a man, that is not news, because it happens so often.
But if a man bites a dog, that is news.

-- John B. Bogart

Firing Fido! describes numerous problems many people have in their careers and lives - the behaviors that often constrain them from getting what they *need*. The primary focus so far has been on dealing with all the behavior obstacles inside us, whether they were Caged Fidos that we have <u>full</u> control over or Uncaged Fidos over which we have <u>partial</u> control, as well as the external *Scooby-Doos* (underperforming best friends). While all the stories have been true, the names and circumstances have been altered to avoid identification and protect peoples' anonymity.

I'd now like to share my own story to illustrate how I dealt with my obstacles and put the principles of this book into practice. Family confrontations are often the most uncomfortable for folks to deal with and most people avoid them at all cost. In my personal life, I faced one of the most difficult Uncaged Fidos of all - a confrontation with my father over a very sensitive subject.

Into The Doghouse (the trouble begins)

My Dad has many admirable qualities. He has always been a very loving and devoted father. He cares deeply for his children, provided well for us, spent a great deal of time with us, educated us and was present at all our activities during our school years. Dad is a faithful partner to my Mom and loyal to a small group of friends.

Like my grandfather Thomas, however, Dad is extremely strong-willed, stubborn and independent. He hates to show any weakness or vulnerability. Like many traditional Greek men, Dad considered himself the domineering patriarch of the house - just as Michael Constantine said in the film *My Big Fat Greek Wedding*, "I am the <u>head</u> of this house." Dad felt compelled to control, a trait he learned from his father and passed down to me. Most people considered Dad a 'control freak'. I'm not including this perception as a judgment of him but simply as an observation of his behaviors. Everyone who knows him says the same thing and they still love him!

In my family upbringing, obedience to Dad was of utmost importance. My parents' marriage is loving and caring as long as Mom does not 'rock the boat'. She realized this long ago and decided to cope with that reality by cooperating and being obedient to his wishes. She has felt happy in a marriage that's lasted 56 years and is still going strong! My Mom, my brother and I were subservient to Dad's will, moods and whims. We always avoided volatile topics and emotional confrontation with Dad to avoid upsetting him. Because we never risked speaking openly and possibly offending him, we never learned how to set healthy boundaries with him or others.

Although he is now in his eighties, my Dad is the poster-boy for good health - a true inspiration to us all. No one his age looks as good or acts as youthfully. He travels constantly and can outpace everyone when, for example, climbing ancient ruins. His doctors rave about the fantastic shape he's in and the fact that he has the body and activity level of a man 20-30 years his junior.

A huge family secret my Dad had sworn us to keep was the fact that he had undergone quadruple bypass heart surgery some years ago. We were not allowed to discuss this situation with <u>any</u> of our relatives or friends. Even though he recovered with flying colors, Dad decreed, "What happens here is nobody's business but our own and you *will* obey my wishes." Although this surgery was very common for a man his age and certainly nothing to be ashamed of, he was adamant that we maintain absolute silence.

My family, when I was growing up, was extremely conscious of keeping any problems within the immediate family. As children, we learned to pretend, keep our mouths shut and suppress our natural need to share ourselves with others in an appropriate manner. Over time, bit by bit, we censored ourselves.

Fido Gets Fed (the price paid for overloyalty)

Years later, a very close friend near my age had undergone a similar surgical procedure as my Dad and was describing his physical therapy to me. It was on the tip of my tongue to say, "Oh, my Dad had a similar experience with that particular post-operative therapy," but I stopped myself cold. Here I was, in my thirties, constrained from having an open and honest conversation with one of my closest friends. Biting my tongue made me feel awkward and uncomfortable. I wasn't even able to disclose how proud I was of Dad and his amazingly quick recovery. I felt coerced into keeping a family secret strictly out of fear of Dad's reaction, which made me feel like a small child who couldn't be trusted.

In addition to impacting my personal relationships, my inability to deal effectively with my ultimate family authority figure - Dad - affected my ability to deal with certain corporate authority figures. Over my entire career, I had a history of problems dealing appropriately with many overpowering and controlling authority figures. I chafed under the collar whenever a leader tried to impose his or her will on me and I often overreacted. My ability to choose my battles was not well-honed, which got in the way of my ability to advance fully in my corporate career. I found myself incessantly battling certain authority figures and not being able to state my own needs in a direct and healthy manner. I realized the more open and honest my relationship was with Dad, the healthier my relationships would be with others - clients, co-workers and authority figures.

Lack of healthy boundary setting with Dad caused another very important work-related issue to creep up. I had never felt free to use the full range of my true natural gifts in my career work, which led to a lack of real happiness, fulfillment and F.U.N. So I decided to research and write *Firing Fido!* and develop a series of supporting workshops to fully incorporate the knowledge gained from my own personal and career discovery process as well as my corporate and consulting experiences. As I started researching and writing, however, I felt frustrated - a huge mental block was in my way. No matter how hard I tried, I felt very hesitant to disclose certain important topics in my writing. I hit such a dry spell that I was forced to stop for a few months. Practically my entire work life and personal life was put on hold until this mental block could be resolved.

Fido Gets Fired (action taken)

I finally decided not to put up with this 'shroud of silence' policy any longer. Enough was enough! Although I thought confronting Dad would be an extremely challenging undertaking, I decided it was something I needed to do. Healthy confrontation was the key to having full freedom in the way I chose to live my life and to get what I needed. I told my Mom, in confidence, that I was going to confront Dad on our family's secrecy policy concerning his heart surgery. She exclaimed, "HOW can you even consider doing that? You know how Dad feels about it. We all should respect his wishes, even if it's difficult for us!" I replied, "I'm sorry. I am no longer willing to give him power over what I can or can't say. This affects my ability to disclose my thoughts and feelings to others - even to my best friends. I won't allow myself to be treated like that any longer." She warned me, "Don't do it! If you do, he may get so angry at you that he may never talk to you again. IS THAT WHAT YOU WANT?"

I fully understood and appreciated her fears. Any time you attempt a major change in your life, most of the people around you - especially the ones who are well-intentioned and love you - are very reluctant to see you change and threaten the status quo. Mom's fears did not dissuade me. I kept silently whispering the words of Janis Joplin, "Don't compromise yourself, honey. You're all you've got." [25] I calmly said to Mom, "I don't believe for a minute that he'll ostracize me. I think deep down he loves his family very much and he wouldn't do anything to get in the way of his love for his children."

My self-doubts, however, started to creep in after the discussion with Mom. I thought to myself, "Why can't I let Dad protect his privacy about his surgery? Why can't I just let sleeping dogs lie? What's the big deal? Just get over it!" Discounting my feelings had always caused me to never give myself permission to view my personal concerns as being important enough to express to others. The messages pounded into my head from my family upbringing made it very clear that 'keeping the peace' in the family was more important than expressing what I needed and felt. I felt stuck.

I said to myself, at that point, "Hold on a second here. My needs matter too! Dad's needs are not the only concern." My primary need was to be able to express myself fully and freely without being controlled by anyone else. Dad's control over my ability to communicate in a healthy way with some of my closest friends was impacting the intimacy of these relationships. This issue also caused my work to suffer due to my inability to disclose important information appropriately in my book writing and to confront other authority figures in a healthy way.

I finally decided to make the meeting of my own *needs* my primary priority in life.

I have dinner with my family - brother, sister-in-law and parents - at my parents' home on many Sunday evenings. At the end of one of these dinners, after establishing an upbeat mood, I summoned the courage to confront Dad in a healthy way. I looked at him and said in a respectful tone, "I want to talk to you about something that's been on my mind for a long time. The topic is your heart surgery and how I have never been allowed to talk about it or your subsequent recovery with anyone outside this room."

The atmosphere in the room immediately became quiet and tense - the air felt so heavy I could hardly breathe. I boldly continued, "This absolute silence still causes me to check myself on what I can say to others. I can't even talk about it happily and tell people how proud I am of the way you came out of it in such good shape." I went on to describe some other negative events that had occurred in my life and the link of this issue to those events.

I continued politely and firmly, "I have two major needs at this point in my life. The first is the ability to express myself fully and freely without being controlled by anyone else. The second is to maintain a good relationship with the people I care about most - my family. The issue of control over free expression has been a long pattern of behavior and it has impacted my life a great deal. Your control over what I can say, and what my reactions are allowed to be, has forced me to demand control over others in my own relationships as well as to censor myself. I don't like the way I have felt about myself all this time. This isn't the way I want to lead my life any longer - it doesn't work for me. My desire is to be happy and to get what I know I deserve in life."

I paused to look at my Dad and the rest of the family around the table - they were all in rapt silence. Dad listened intently and motioned for me to continue. I said calmly and directly, "If this was just about your wishes and didn't involve anyone else, then that would be perfectly all right. This intrudes, however, on my ability to get what I need - to have open and healthy interpersonal relationships. It's something, therefore, that I can't accept any longer. Some wishes are reasonable and some wishes are unreasonable - there's a difference. I'm putting this topic out there for you to consider and think about. This is about what I need to live a happier and healthier life. What I need from you is your love, your support and your encouragement. You mean a whole lot to me. This is the new way I'm going to live my life and my life will change. I'd rather have you with me than not with me. I'm asking for your love and support in my quest for a new and balanced life."

My Dad responded wonderfully, saying, "I want you to feel free to say whatever you want to whomever you want. You explained things very clearly and very well. I'm sorry that you took so long to bring this up to me if it was bothering you so much. I wish you had brought these things up many years ago and not held them back for so long, so we could have dealt with them constructively at that time. You have my full support to discuss whatever you would like about this topic or any other. We should all strive for open and honest communication." The palpable tension in the room deflated like a balloon and everyone at the table relaxed. We went on to discuss some other related topics and everything was fine.

Paws To Reflect - Counterproductive Steps (key lessons)

My Dad was correct. I *had* waited too long to confront him regarding important issues. One of the less than optimal relationship lessons I learned from Mom growing up was to put a greater premium on 'keeping the peace' than on expressing my own needs to others. Mom grew up in a household where the husband worked and the wife stayed home to raise the children. She, like most women of her generation, was neither expected nor urged to get a college education. She was encouraged to be a homemaker and marry well. Mom had chosen well, in her case, and married a responsible, ambitious, religious, well-educated man who was interested in traveling around the world. Both of them were raised in traditional Greek families and Dad considered his primary job to be meeting the family's material needs. I always felt that Dad viewed emotional support within the family as being more Mom's responsibility than his own.

Although my Mom truly loves my Dad and has always been happy in her relationship with him, her view of *happiness* equated with cooperation and obedience to his wishes in order to 'keep the peace'. As long as Dad was loving and faithful, provided well for the family with a secure job, wasn't physically abusive and didn't drink or gamble, she didn't complain. She felt grateful that all her material and marital fidelity needs were met. This definition of *happiness* was passed down to me but, unfortunately, it limited my expectations of what I thought I deserved in my own relationships. I intellectually understood the difference in viewpoints between my parent's generation and my own generation but I didn't fully grasp the emotional impact on me. This prolonged my inability to view <u>my emotional needs as being equally important as my other needs</u>.

Paws To Reflect - Productive Steps (key lessons)

Like all loving parents, my parents did what they thought was best for their children. I'm not sharing this story to be disparaging of them in any way. I am very proud of my Dad, in fact, and happy he's done so well since his heart surgery. He truly is a great physical specimen.

Standing up to Dad took courage and involved taking an emotional risk. My Mom's concerns about the possible outcomes of confronting Dad only added to my own fears. One of the most difficult things to do is to express your innermost needs to a person who has the power to hurt you emotionally. We usually have the greatest difficulty dealing openly and honestly with the people closest to us. I didn't know for sure how it would turn out and I had to let go of the result.

Firing my major Uncaged Fido of 'keeping the peace at all cost' in my family life allowed me to overcome my self-imposed limitation of fear and reap the rewards. Since my confrontation was done in a very healthy manner, Dad and I were able to move on successfully. No ill will was generated. Telling my perception of the truth via healthy confrontation improved my ability to communicate clearly what I needed and set healthy boundaries. My relationship with both Dad and Mom actually improved. We now have a closer, more honest and healthy relationship than we did before. Rather than hiding, we tell each other the truth as we perceive it using appropriate boundaries. We are able to discuss deeper topics and disclose more openly than before.

My Dad, in fact, had no qualms with my open disclosure of everything revealed in this chapter to the readers of this book. He encouraged me to resume writing *Firing Fido!* and both he and Mom actively contributed to the book editing process.

While not perfect, of course, my family and I are moving in the proper direction. Changing ingrained habits, behaviors and beliefs developed over hundreds of years of family tradition doesn't happen overnight - we're still learning and improving. My Mom also learned from this experience that she didn't have to approach life from the standpoint of constantly worrying. Healthy confrontation allows people to resolve issues without resorting to either yelling or giving each other 'the silent treatment'.

...Healthy Confrontation Allows Career To Progress

After the healthy confrontation with Dad, my muzzle had been removed. The writing for the book and workshops began to flow again. The eye of the tiger had returned! I was able to disclose fully and communicate my ideas - no longer trapped by overallegiance to a 'family script' that was getting in my way. The *life* confrontation allowed me to move forward and progress in my *work*. I broke through the walls of my self-imposed maze of major obstacles to get to the other side - to follow my bliss and achieve happiness, fulfillment and F.U.N.

The secrecy over Dad's heart surgery was just the tip of the iceberg - there was so much more than that. I wasn't focused on just this one issue - it was representative of a much larger issue. Things such as keeping seemingly innocuous family secrets, taken individually, might not seem like such a big deal but they tend to pile up over time. I knew if I didn't say something now about this subject, then I may hold back later about a more important topic. Major trouble would occur eventually - maybe not now but at some point in the future. The heart surgery issue was simply the breaking point for me.

The most automatic obstacles are the inherited ideas in our head that came from how we were raised and taught to believe. An unchallenged parental authority figure can set up many of the difficulties people have in doing what they really desire to do in their lives. The strong family script embedded in my head caused me to think I was doing something *very* wrong if I operated contrary to the family rules. The family is where I learned 'not to confront' in my personal life.

The family institution is one of the most intimidating structures for many people to overcome. My historical inability to deal with an overpowering parental authority figure led to my inability to confront in a healthy way while in my thirties. I had been controlled by unresolved conflicts with Dad. I feared, even as an adult, getting figuratively *smacked* if I confronted him. I also wound up *smacking* myself by incorporating my Mom's concern and fearing that Dad's core love was going to be withdrawn if I challenged the family rules. That fear caused me to hold back for many years.

Everyone brings family issues into the workplace. I realized if I didn't solve my own family issues, then it would be very difficult to deal with related workplace issues. I had to modify my own behavior to improve an important situation in my life. Personal growth starts in our own home, usually, and then evolves into changes made in the workplace. There's a clear link between my ability to break a less than optimal family script and my ability to make better professional decisions.

Not all families, of course, are like my family. Almost *everyone*, however, has some kind of fear or obstacle to deal with in order to develop, grow and get what he or she needs. It could be a confrontation with a father, mother, spouse, friend, religious leader, manager or co-worker. It could be the fear of taking a financial risk or the fear of independence and living alone. The possibilities are endless.

I definitely needed to undergo a radical redefinition of loyalty in order to unleash my true self-leadership. I was overloyal to the desires of others - my Dad, the organization I worked for and the projects I managed - putting them ahead of my own needs. I had a poor work/life balance since I often took on other peoples' responsibilities. My main shift was to determine my needs and be loyal to these needs being met first.

I enjoyed the research and writing of this book and incorporated the knowledge I gained into my personal life as well as my consulting practice. Although it wasn't always easy, I faced my fears through unyielding introspection and transformed my own life in many ways. I first analyzed and understood the impacts of my own family script on my adult life. I honestly reflected on certain actions in my past and scrupulously analyzed why they worked or didn't work. I began by taking *baby steps* and made specific changes in my life.

Before confronting my Dad, I also started dealing effectively with the major Caged Fidos that were taking me off the path of becoming the unique individual I was created to be. I forced myself, eventually, to step *far* outside my comfort zone. These changes regarded how I managed my drive, my analytic skills and approach to money, my connection with children and animals and my creative skills. My political and spiritual viewpoints also broadened greatly.

...Have F.U.N.

Radically redefining loyalty is the way to make our jobs and lives more F.U.N. - to be able to do more creative, productive and energetic work. Remember . . . energy fuels action! To paraphrase the Dalai Lama, 'No one else can liberate us, we can only liberate ourselves'. Everything I needed was always within me but I needed to remove my own self-imposed obstacles. I had to trust my intuition, articulate my vision for myself, own it and then act on it . . . and all these things occurred because . . .

I Fired My Own Fidos!

BARKING UP
THE RIGHT TREE

A Last Wag
(Summary of major Fido principles)

Everyone has observed how much more dogs are animated when they hunt in a pack, than when they pursue their game apart.
We might, perhaps, be at a loss to explain this phenomenon, if we had not experience of a similar in ourselves.

-- David Hume

Fido obstacles are things to which we've become overattached. They have a dog pack mentality - self-led, a bit on the wild side and running on instinct. Your Fidos are likely driving *you*, you aren't driving them. You might have let a dog or two in the house. As far as Fido is concerned, he's the most important thing in your house. He is starting to get in the way. Fido has found his way into the refrigerator and into the garbage. He has started to invite some of his friends over as well.

To set yourself free, *you* need to liberate yourself from yourself. We have all been allegiant to something or someone that we put ahead of ourselves - to our own detriment. What's in your way of acting in your own best interest? What obstacles are you creating for yourself based on self-defeating and unproductive thought patterns? What outdated beliefs, assumptions and practices do you have? The real limits are largely self-constructed and in our own minds. Nelson Mandela said:

"We ask ourselves, 'Who am I to be brilliant, gorgeous, talented, fabulous?' Actually, who are you not to be? . . . Your playing small doesn't serve the world. There's nothing enlightened about shrinking so that other people won't feel insecure around you. . . . as we let our light shine, we consciously give other people permission to do the same. As we are liberated from our own fear, our presence automatically liberates others." [26]

Many people are distracted and lack focus. What are you focused on? Are you moving in the direction you desire? Or are you staying very busy but going nowhere? Where you place your focus is the most valuable thing you can do. Power exists in focus, choice and commitment - making specific decisions and acting on them. Knowing what *not* to do is just as important as what to do. The definition of powerlessness is simply wishing and dreaming - being open to all possibilities and options but not choosing.

During the golden age of animation of the 1940s and 1950s, Disney was the land of enchantment and wishing (e.g., Jiminy Cricket in *Pinocchio*) and Warner Brothers was the land of personal empowerment (e.g., Bugs Bunny outwitting Elmer Fudd). Which do you choose? It's great to have dreams but they have limited value unless followed by action. Commitment is the working definition of success - moving from the land of enchantment into the land of personal empowerment.

The concepts of *Firing Fido!* are universal human principles and are applicable to anyone at any level of an organization. **Personal accountability is about holding yourself accountable for your own thinking and behaviors and the results they produce. You can only change yourself - you can't change anyone else.**

If you want more and better personal satisfaction and happiness and a more enjoyable career, then you have to change something. Change is the key to growing, creating and adapting. Most people say they want to change but they don't want to do anything differently. It doesn't work that way! Personal growth includes insight *and* behavior change; insight alone is never enough.[27]   You have to change certain key behaviors in order to get what you need. The 1970s musical group *America* sang, "Oz never did give nothing to the Tin Man that he didn't already have." [28]   You have the power to think differently and act differently - it's inside you right now.

You, like most adults, probably spend about 75 percent of your adult waking time doing work-related activities - getting ready for work, traveling to work, working, contemplating work and decompressing after work.[29] Removing the Fidos that are getting in your way leads you to personal expression and career enjoyment - the Emerald City on the other side of the rainbow. Imagine yourself doing exactly what you love doing - composing, drawing, engineering, designing - the list is endless. During what activity does time seem to be nonexistent, and when you finish, you feel immeasurably fulfilled? Enjoying your work helps you feel better - happier, calmer, more satisfied and energized. You are best at what you do effortlessly and what comes most naturally, not at what you have to work at the hardest. Can you picture living in that world? . . . Ahhhhhhhhhhhhhhh!

Do not underestimate, however, your brain's resistance to change. Human beings build confidence a step at a time, changing by gradual stages, especially when it comes to emotionally loaded issues. No one learns how to swim by cliff diving! Richard Dreyfuss said to Bill Murray in the film *What About Bob?*, "It means setting small, reasonable goals for yourself - one day at a time, one tiny step at a time . . . *baby steps.*" You may only have to do a few things differently in order to have a powerful effect. Narrow down an area of improvement to just one specific behavior. Take it to the smallest, tiniest level you can and start changing there. Exhibit that behavior differently than you did before. It will give you the confidence and the competence to continue. Changing ingrained habits and behaviors may be some of the most important work you've ever done but will take some time. Don't get discouraged. It's okay to make mistakes and learn from them. Give yourself permission to fail and continue to move forward.

We *all* need to undergo a radical redefinition of loyalty in order to unleash our true self-leadership. Many of the stories in *Firing Fido!* are dramatic - some are funny and bittersweet - and all are true. Since we all overuse something, I invite you to consider which of these Caged and Uncaged Fidos apply to your life. By first dealing with the internal Caged Fidos you fully control, you'll be able to deal more effectively with the internal Uncaged Fidos you partially control, as well as the external *Scooby-Doos* (underperforming best friends). Fidos are the root cause of what may be in your way of taking personal accountability and ownership for your actions and behaviors. They are the obstacles in the way of getting what you need and having F.U.N. at work. Remember . . . **F**iring **U**nleashes your e**N**ergy and energy fuels action! Robert Frost wrote:

> Two roads diverged in a wood, and I -
> I took the one less traveled by,
> And that has made all the difference.[30]

At least two roads are always in front of you. One is the road that you know, the one you've been on for your entire life. There's another road - the path to your essence, to your power, to your true identity and to your needs. I encourage you to step out and be *yourself* - in order to have F.U.N. in your career and life. If you say, "Why start now?" then my reply is, "if not now, when?" In the words of former *Washington Post* publisher Katharine Graham, "To love what you do and feel that it matters - how could anything be more fun?" [31]

Join Me. Start By Firing Your Own Fidos!

LAST BUT NOT LEASH

(Appendices)

DEFINITION OF TERMS

Many terms in *Firing Fido!* are used in a different way than many people are accustomed to seeing them. A new understanding of these terms is necessary in order to apply the book's principles effectively:

Term	*Firing Fido!* Usage
CONFRONTATION / RELATIONSHIP TERMS	
Healthy Confrontation (pp. 4-5)	-INTERNAL: Firing any bad habits to which we've become attached. -EXTERNAL: Delivering hard news to others in a truthful and respectful way when making tough decisions. [Conventional wisdom usually encourages coping with situations via avoidance and denial.]
Healthy Working Relationship (pp. 4-5)	Mutual and honest self-disclosure of information and trust. The goal is 'to know and to be known'. [Healthy working relationships are usually defined as remaining *comfortable* and making sure we know more about the other person than we let them know about us.]
Leading (p. 69)	Understanding how to make the tough decisions and confronting in a healthy way when necessary - it's about commitment and decisiveness.
FIDO TERMS	
Fido (pp. vi, 15)	Obstacle - overloyalty or misplaced loyalty to a person, belief or habit.
Caged Fido (p. 1)	Obstacle we wrestle with internally that we fully control.
Uncaged Fido (p. 1)	Obstacle we wrestle with internally that we partially control.
Fatal Fido (p. 28)	More concerned with being liked first and respected second. This behavior causes practically every other problem to get worse.
Alpha Dog (p. 67)	First person establishing dominance in a role tends to keep it.
GILLIGAN / SCOOBY TERMS	
True Gilligan (p. 114)	Underperforming best friend - adds minimal to no value while being clearly destructive. Keeps a wide variety of other people from doing what's in their own and the company's best interest.
Situational Gilligan (p. 113)	Person who knows his job as long as the situation remains a regular, comfortable, day-to-day routine. He is fine until pushed - then he gets overwhelmed and becomes destructive - a passive-aggressive resister.
Scooby (p. 114)	Underperforming best friend - a headache to endure, causes numerous problems and delays the ultimate solutions. Tends to come through, however, in the end and gets the job done in spite of himself.

Term	*Firing Fido!* Usage
INTEGRITY TERMS	
Honesty and Truth Telling (p. 108)	Highest and purest form of respect (as well as the most precious gift) we give another person - when done in an appropriate manner.
F.U.N. (pp. 3-4)	**F**iring **U**nleashes e**N**ergy - the intrinsic satisfaction of doing fulfilling, rewarding and enjoyable work that is linked to our true identity and what we do best. This is the F.U.N. that gets good work DONE!
LOYALTY TERMS	
Healthy Loyalty (pp. vi, 2)	Becoming aware of our own needs and making the meeting of these needs our primary priority. [Traditionally defined as being faithful to a person, cause, ideal, custom, institution or product.]
Lopsided Loyalty (pp. vi, 15)	[Same definition as *Fido*.]
Overloyalty (p. 3)	Putting the needs and wants of others ahead of our own needs, even if it's only a minimum of 51 percent focused on others and a maximum of 49 percent focused on ourselves.
Misplaced Loyalty (p. 3)	Having faith in a harmful ideology or substance to get us through the day.
PSYCHOLOGICAL TERMS	
Addiction (pp. 40, 44)	Any process, activity or substance that takes over our lives and controls us. Addictions work best in secret and in isolation.
Denial (p. 41)	Basic defense mechanism of addiction. If we deny the existence of the addiction, then we can avoid dealing with it. The things we resist, however, tend to persist and get worse over time.
Boundary (p. 6)	How far we can go with comfort in a relationship. A guideline to help us clarify the limits of acceptable behavior.
Needs (p. vii)	Our basic rights as human beings.
Wants (p. vii)	Our own desires.
Family Script (p. 27)	Way we view the world - our system of beliefs and assumptions – based on how we were brought up and taught to think by our families.
Baby Steps (p. 139)	Setting small, reasonable goals for ourselves - one tiny step at a time.

Please refer to pages 79-81, 86-88 or 128-129 for a variety of specific approaches and phrases to choose from when confronting a difficult person in your life in a healthy way.
Choose ones that are most relevant to your own situation and be sure to look at phrase usage within the context of the story. Each story, of course, contains a different set of circumstances.

SUPPORT GROUP INFORMATION

Addictions are any processes, activities or substances that take over a person's life and control him or her. Addictions work best in secret and in isolation and lead to self-defeating behaviors. All sorts of unhealthy consequences flow from addictions.

Denial is the basic defense mechanism of addiction - if something doesn't exist, then it doesn't need to be dealt with. The bad news, however, is that the things people resist tend to persist and get worse over time.

The philosophy of addiction provides a sound theoretical framework to help people deal with the negative aspect of the portion of their personality that becomes compulsive. Understanding the underlying principles of addiction helps people raise their issues to the surface and develop effective strategies for dealing with them.

All addictions are enabled by and follow the identical psychological cycle of perpetuation. Workaholics (work addicts) often have myriad addictions. Their primary addiction is to work and they may also have secondary addictions to substances or other processes/activities. The secondary addictions act as crutches and smokescreens, which allow their denial system to remain intact. The following support groups provide a safe opportunity to get help and begin a recovery process by getting together with folks who share similar issues.

Process/Activity Addictions:

Work Addict:
Workaholics Anonymous
World Service Organization
P.O. Box 289
Menlo Park, CA 94026 USA
Phone: (510) 273-9253
www.workaholics-anonymous.org

Business Debt Addict:
Debtors Anonymous
General Service Office
P.O. Box 920888
Needham, MA 02492 USA
Phone: (781) 453-2743
www.debtorsanonymous.org/
BusinessDA.htm   or
www.solvency.org/bda.html

Gambling Addict:
Gamblers Anonymous
International Service Office
P.O. Box 17173
Los Angeles, CA 90017 USA
Phone: (213) 386-8789
www.gamblersanonymous.org

Personal Debt Addict:
Debtors Anonymous
General Service Office
P.O. Box 920888
Needham, MA 02492 USA
Phone: (781) 453-2743
www.debtorsanonymous.org

Sex Addict:
Sexaholics Anonymous
International Central Office
P.O. Box 3565
Brentwood, TN 37024 USA
Phone: (615) 370-6062
www.sa.org

Emotions Addict:
(Depression, Bipolar, etc.)
Emotions Anonymous
International
P.O. Box 4245
St. Paul, MN 55104 USA
Phone: (651) 647-9712
www.emotionsanonymous.org

Other process/activity addictions include rageaholics (anger addicts), shopaholics (shopping and buying addicts), exerciseaholics (exercise addicts), etc.

Substance Addictions:

Alcohol Addict:
Alcoholics Anonymous
World Services, Inc.
Grand Central Station
P.O. Box 459
New York, NY 10163 USA
Phone: (212) 870-3400
www.aa.org

Drug Addict:
Narcotics Anonymous
World Service Office
P.O. Box 9999
Van Nuys, CA 91409 USA
Phone: (818) 773-9999
www.na.org

Smoking Addict (Nicotine):
Nicotine Anonymous
World Services
419 Main Street, PMB#370
Huntington Beach, CA 92648 USA
Phone: (415) 750-0328
www.nicotine-anonymous.org

Food Addict:
(Salt, Sugar, Caffeine,
Carbohydrates, etc.)
Overeaters Anonymous
World Service Office
P.O. Box 44020
Rio Rancho, NM 87174 USA
Phone: (505) 891-2664
www.oa.org

The major support groups available for both substance and process/activity addictions are highlighted in this section. All contact information is current as of the time of book publication. There are literally hundreds of other specialized support groups in existence. Please check your local library or newspaper for a comprehensive listing of groups and meetings in your area.

SHARE IT WITH OTHERS

Firing Fido! makes a meaningful tool for colleagues and a terrific gift for friends. To order copies please logon to www.FiringFido.com or send a copy of this form:

QUANTITY

_____ *Firing Fido!* by Chris Kozakis $17.00 ($22.15 Canadian)

Payable in U.S. funds only. Book price: $17.00 each copy. We accept Visa, Mastercard, American Express, Discover ($10.00 min.), checks or money orders payable to **The Kozakis Companies** ($15.00 fee for returned checks). No Cash/COD. In U.S./Canada call toll-free (866) 700-5113 [International call (602) 331-0334], fax (602) 331-0361 or mail orders to:

The Kozakis Companies   **Bill my**
7000 North 16th Street   credit card #_____exp.____
Suite 120#461   ___Visa ___MC ___AMEX ___Discover
Phoenix, AZ 85020-5547   **Signature**_____**Date**_____
U.S.A.   __Fee enclosed. Check/Money Order #_____
                  __Signed Purchase Order attached P.O.#_____

Bill to_____
Address_____ Book Total $____
City_____State_____Zip_____
Daytime Phone # (_____) _____ Sales Tax (if applicable) $____
Email_____
Ship to_____ Shipping & Handling $____
Address_____
City_____State_____Zip_____ Total Amount Due $____

State of Arizona residents please add 8.1 percent sales tax ($1.38 for a single book).

Shipping & Handling:
- U.S. $3.49 for one book ($0.99 each additional book).
  Canada $5.49 for one book ($2.49 each additional book).
- For Express Mailing or International ordering options,
  logon to www.FiringFido.com.
- Please allow 4-6 weeks for U.S./Canada delivery.
  Please allow 6-8 weeks for International delivery.

Offer subject to change without notice.

ABOUT THE AUTHOR

Chris Kozakis is an expert on self-development within business workplace settings. He is an independent consultant with seasoned business experience from many perspectives - including strategic planning, reengineering, quality, project management and information technology. Chris also founded and ran one of the first personal computer training businesses in the Southwestern United States. He managed all aspects of the business, ranging from sales to service delivery.

Chris' Strategic Management Consulting approach applies the principles of healthy confrontation and personal accountability to both organizational transformation and people transformation. Chris incorporates timeless wisdom and inspiration with practical business application based on over 15 years of corporate and consulting experience in the real world of work.

Chris has management consulting, information technology consulting, line management and executive level experience with American Express and other Fortune 500, mid-size and startup companies. His education includes a Master of Business Administration (M.B.A.) degree in Strategic Planning from the University of California at Berkeley and a Bachelor of Science (B.S.) degree in Computer Information Systems from Arizona State University.

Chris resides in Phoenix, Arizona.

WANT TO KNOW MORE?
...About Organizational Transformation

Want to become an indispensable market leader by using the *Firing Fido!* principles of healthy confrontation and personal accountability? Want to strategically build or reengineer your organization for revolutionary improvement? Then contact Chris Kozakis for his organizational consulting services to help your company make changes for both short-term success and long-term sustained value.

Success is measured by achieving robust profit margins, increased productivity, improved efficiency and reduced expenses that result from crisp execution and unsurpassed performance. Flexible, adaptable and stronger work teams foster a radically empowered workforce that responds quickly to unprecedented change and rapidly evolving customer requirements. A high-morale climate based on employee responsibility truly unleashes the enormous reservoir of untapped initiative, creativity and energy that already exists within your employees.

Chris' new approach and practical tools help ensure organizations become simpler and easier to lead in today's frenzied and fast-paced global economy. His principles help leaders implement overall organizational strategy in the most effective manner possible - by making **choices** and **decisions** simpler and clearer to understand.

These improvement concepts apply wherever people get together as a group to try to get something done. These include all types of organizations: business, government, non-profit organizations, education, etc. Chris' concepts also apply to all functions (i.e., Customer Service, Information Technology, Sales & Marketing, Human Resources & Training, etc.).

WANT TO KNOW MORE?
...About People Transformation

Want to find a way for your staff to discover and experience the *Firing Fido!* principles of healthy confrontation and personal accountability? Then contact Chris for coaching or one of his high-energy workshops on leadership and teamwork.

Using entertaining and hands-on approaches, Chris will help you transform the playful, yet profound, messages of *Firing Fido!* into practical action that energizes your day-to-day work life. Discover your true power and potential, radically improve your personal effectiveness and escape from your own traps by having more F.U.N.!

Discover powerful influencing strategies to navigate the emotional, political and cultural climate of your organization in a balanced manner with integrity. Learn how to leverage your skills more effectively and improve your ability to communicate - to manage perceptions and expectations when dealing with difficult people and contentious situations. You can learn how to take initiative, manage your career more successfully in your current organization and advance to the extent you desire.

Learn the two most important leadership challenges - 1) how to focus and 2) how to make the tough decisions - using a variety of direct truth telling and flexible problem solving principles. Become aware of the obstacles that are getting in your way. Focus on specific tools and techniques for how to deal better with barriers. Use customized action plans to practice **changed behaviors** to overcome these obstacles. Learn by doing!

Chris' organizational consulting services and workshops may be utilized at any location around the world, and can be customized for your needs. If you'd like more details, please stop by and visit on the Internet at www.FiringFido.com Additionally, the website will discuss other interesting real-life examples, which do not appear in the book, such as dealing with outdated policies and technical systems. If you have any questions, comments or stories of your own, please contact him at **Chris@ChrisKozakis.com** or call toll-free in U.S./Canada at (866) 700-5113 or Internationally at (602) 331-0334.

ACKNOWLEDGMENTS

Five years ago, I could not have envisioned writing this book. Then again, five years ago I was not the same person I am today. I would like to thank Tom Kurtz (professional development advisor) and Arnold Lopez (personal development advisor) for helping me to achieve my life vision. Tom's help has been priceless through his roles as mentor/coach, visionary, discovery facilitator, contention manager, content expert, editor and friend. Tom helped me to discover what I enjoy doing the most and am best at doing. Arnold helped me to understand and overcome my own obstacles to having my best possible life experience.

My thanks especially to Rick Wandrych and Tony Sola, as well as to Scott Ferris, Rob Fallows and Mike Kublin, for their support and help in reviewing and editing my manuscript. Particular thanks to Emma Melikian for seeing the creative force in me many years ago and encouraging me to pursue it. Thanks to Richard Cousins and Scott Mooneyham for teaching me many of these principles during my career.

Also thanks to Ray Momary, Rob Melikian, Ramona Visconti, Nevine Melikian, Jim Melikian and Glenn Cunningham, as well as to all of the 'Kozaki' - Tina, John, Ken and Ellen - for their constant support and encouragement. To all of my friends - I apologize for not spending as much time with you in the past few years as I would have preferred. This was a time of intense personal transformation, incredible change and required unyielding focus. If I have hurt anyone, I truly do apologize - it wasn't intentional!

Lastly, thanks to the spirit of discovery I received from the two true Renaissance men I have had the privilege to know in my life - in memory of Bill Tatom and Metropolitan Vladimir Nagosky. Time spent with them had an everlasting impact on me.

To Mom - 'Tina' - Katherine Helen Boulakes Kozakis:
- Who modeled love, friendship, empathy, understanding and care

To Dad - John Thomas Kozakis:
- Who modeled doing what he loved to do for a career so that it was never really *work*
- Who taught how to think independently, challenge convention and focus on the root cause of issues and institutions
- Who showed that anything in life was possible by his drive, commitment and determination, while shepherding a bill through the U.S. Congress as an individual citizen

Both have lived (and continue to live) their lives to the fullest and have inspired me to reach for the stars to bring my message to the world

NOTES

1   *Merriam-Webster's Collegiate Dictionary.* Springfield, Massachusetts: Merriam-Webster, Inc. (1993, Tenth Edition): 691.

2   Chu, Chin-Ning. *Do Less, Achieve More: Discover the Hidden Power of Giving In.* New York: Regan Books (1998): 141.

3   Whitfield, Charles L., M.D. *Boundaries and Relationships: Knowing, Protecting and Enjoying the Self.* Deerfield Beach, Florida: Health Communications, Inc. (1993): 1.

4   Gamble, Kenny, Huff, Leon and Jackson, A. (The O'Jays). Song: "For the Love of Money." Album: *Ship Ahoy.* Sony (1973).

5   Senge, Peter M. *The Fifth Discipline: The Art & Practice of The Learning Organization.* New York: Currency Doubleday (1994): 54. (Note: Originally published 1990).

6   Holmes, W. (The Hues Corporation). Song: "Rock The Boat." Album: *The Very Best Of The Hues Corporation.* BMG Entertainment (1998). (Note: Originally recorded 1973).

7   Halpern, Howard M. *Cutting Loose: An Adult's Guide to Coming to Terms with Your Parents.* New York: Fireside (1990). (Note: Originally published 1976).

8   Napier, Augustus Y. with Whitaker, Carl A., M.D. *The Family Crucible: The Intense Experience of Family Therapy.* New York: Quill (2002). (Note: Originally published 1978).

9   Bradshaw, John. *Bradshaw On: The Family - A New Way of Creating Solid Self-Esteem*. Deerfield Beach, Florida: Health Communications, Inc. (1996). (Note: Originally published 1988).

10 Beckwith, Harry. *Selling The Invisible: A Field Guide to Modern Marketing*. New York: Warner Books, Inc. (1997): 6.

11 Kelman, Ellen. "Men's Fears: What Psychologists Hear Most Often." In *Arizona Healthy Living* magazine (March/April 1998): 34.

12 Yate, Martin. *Hiring the Best: A Manager's Guide to Effective Interviewing*. Holbrook, Massachusetts: Adams Media Corporation (1994). (Note: Originally published 1993).

13 Dauten, Dale. *The Gifted Boss: How to Find, Create and Keep Great Employees*. New York: William Morrow and Company, Inc. (1999): 7.

14 Hart, John. "Success in jobs and grades consume students' lives." In *Kansas State eCollegian* (October 4, 1994, Vol. 99B). Manhattan, Kansas: Kansas State University Student Publications Inc. (Internet excerpt).

15 Peters, Tom and Austin, Nancy. *A Passion For Excellence: The Leadership Difference*. New York: Warner Books, Inc. (1986): 495-496. (Note: Originally published 1985).

16 Beckwith, Harry. *Selling The Invisible: A Field Guide to Modern Marketing*. New York: Warner Books, Inc. (1997): 79.

17 "Inaugural Addresses of the Presidents of the United States." In *Bartleby.com* (2001). New York (Internet excerpt). (Originally given January 20, 1961).

18 Senge, Peter M. *The Fifth Discipline: The Art & Practice of The Learning Organization.* New York: Currency Doubleday (1994): 139. (Note: Originally published 1990).

19 Bermont, Hubert. *How to Become a Successful Consultant in Your Own Field.* Rocklin, California: Prima Publishing (1997): 162. (Note: Originally published 1991).

20 Covey, Stephen R. *The Seven Habits of Highly Effective People: Powerful Lessons in Personal Change.* New York: Fireside (1990): 145. (Note: Originally published 1989).

21 Peck, M. Scott, M.D. *The Road Less Traveled: A New Psychology of Love, Traditional Values and Spiritual Growth.* New York: Touchstone (1998): 153. (Note: Originally published 1978).

22 *Discipline Without Punishment* videotape. Carlsbad, California: CRM Learning (1994).

23 Lerner, Harriet. *The Dance of Intimacy: A Woman's Guide to Courageous Acts of Change in Key Relationships.* New York: Harper Perennial (1990): 86. (Note: Originally published 1989).

24 Charan, Ram and Colvin, Geoffrey. "Why CEOs Fail: It's rarely for lack of smarts or vision. Most unsuccessful CEOs stumble because of one simple, fatal shortcoming." In *Fortune* magazine (June 21, 1999, Vol. 139, No. 12): 69-70.

25 Peters, Tom. *Reinventing Work: The Brand You 50 or: Fifty Ways to Transform Yourself from an "Employee" into a Brand that Shouts Distinction, Commitment, and Passion!* New York: Alfred A. Knopf, Inc. (2001): 3. (Note: Originally published 1999).

26 Rolheiser, Ron. "Real and False Humility." In *Lifeissues.net* (August 5, 2001). Kochi, Japan (Internet excerpt).

27 Bloomfield, Harold H., M.D. with Felder, Leonard. *Making Peace With Your Parents: The Key to Enriching Your Life and All Your Relationships.* New York: Ballantine Books (1996): 133. (Note: Originally published 1983).

28 Bunnell, Dewey (America). Song: "Tin Man." Album: *Holiday.* Warner Bros. (1974).

29 Blanchard, Ken. Foreword to *Fish!: A Remarkable Way to Boost Morale and Improve Results* by Lundin, Stephen C., Paul, Harry and Christensen, John. New York: Hyperion (2000): 9-10.

30 Dyer, Wayne W., Dr. *You'll See It When You Believe It: The Way to Your Personal Transformation.* New York: Avon Books (1990): 36-37. (Note: Originally published 1989).

31 Barkman, Linda J. "Comment." In *Phoenix Home & Garden* magazine (January 1999, Vol. 19, No. 1): 14.

NO DOGS WERE HARMED
IN THE WRITING OF THIS BOOK!

Best Friends Animal Sanctuary

Best Friends Animal Sanctuary is the first and largest 'no kill' animal shelter in the United States. It is a sanctuary for abused and abandoned animals, working to bring about a time when there are no more homeless pets. The sanctuary is home, on any given day, to about 1,500 dogs, cats and other animals from all over the country. Best Friends manages a model campaign, working with shelters and humane groups, to ensure every healthy companion animal that's ever born can be guaranteed a loving, caring home.

This organization is a prime example of exhibiting the principle of treating all other living beings with respect. The work of Best Friends is supported entirely through the donations of its members. Through the generous hearts and hands of everyday people, they can ensure animals who come into the care of Best Friends will never again be alone, hungry, sick, afraid or in pain. As a pet owner myself, I invite you to join me in making a tax-deductible donation to this fine organization. A portion of my book sales will be donated as well. Kindness to animals builds a better world for all of us!

Best Friends Animal Sanctuary
5001 Angel Canyon Road
Kanab, UT 84741 USA
Phone: (435) 644-2001
Email: Info@BestFriends.org
Website:www.BestFriends.org

13229241R00096

Made in the USA
Lexington, KY
20 January 2012